W9-DAY-584

DATE DUE

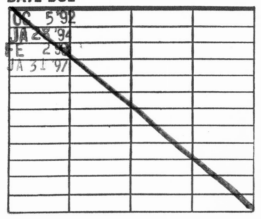

OC 5 '92		
JA 28 '94		
FE 2 9		
JA 31 '97		

DEMCO

PITT SERIES IN POLICY AND
INSTITUTIONAL STUDIES

The Politics

★ of the ★

U.S. Cabinet

REPRESENTATION IN
THE EXECUTIVE BRANCH,
1789–1984

JEFFREY E. COHEN

UNIVERSITY OF PITTSBURGH PRESS

Published by the University of Pittsburgh Press, Pittsburgh, Pa., 15260
Copyright © 1988, University of Pittsburgh Press
All rights reserved
Feffer and Simons, Inc., London
Manufactured in the United States of America

LIBRARY OF CONGRESS CATALOGING-IN-PUBLICATION DATA

Cohen, Jeffrey E.
    The politics of the U.S. Cabinet.

    (Pitt series in policy and institutional studies)
    Bibliography: p. 193.
    Includes index.
        1. Cabinet officers—United States—History. I. Title.
II. Series.
JK611.C64 1988   353.04   88-176
    ISBN 0-8229-3584-8

To my father's memory

Contents

Tables and Figures

Acknowledgments

It is trite for authors to suggest that their works are actually the works of many people and organizations. Yet, however trite, this saying is true. Hence, I want to thank the many people and organizations that helped me in this project. First, I want to acknowledge the Earhart Foundation, which provided me with financial support at a crucial stage. Also, I am grateful to the *American Journal of Political Science,* which has kindly granted me permission to use material that was previously published in its pages (August 1986, 507–16) and makes up parts of chapter 6.

A number of people merit singling out. First, while I was a graduate student at the University of Michigan, George Grassmuck inspired me and many of my cohort to study the executive branch of government. My initial interest in this topic thus goes back to those years long past yet still fresh in my memory. Second, Herbert Weisberg's 1980 convention paper showed me one way to study the cabinet quantitatively and systematically. In the ensuing years conversations and traded papers with Herb have provided me with encouragement and new ways to think about the problem that I tackle in this book. A number of other people deserve special mention for their help, time, comments, and support: Tom Gais, Bert Rockman, Steve Shull, and Greg Brunk. Early discussions with Tom and a paper by him quietly inspired me.

Bert encouraged me to work on this project and early on thought it a worthy endeavor. Steve read the manuscript and associated papers, provided many useful comments, and conveniently had an office just down the hall. Greg spent much time on the phone with me long distance, often at his own expense, listening, commenting, criticizing, and helping. Lastly, special thanks go to David Nice. David not only read the whole manuscript but also showed me the way by publishing a book first. May other people be as lucky as I have been in having a friend like David.

The Politics of
the U.S. Cabinet

Introduction

This book is about the U.S. cabinet. One may ask, Why a book on the cabinet? The cabinet as a body is relatively powerless. It has no corporate responsibility, no ability to enforce decisions. Compared to the Congress, the Supreme Court, or its direct superior, the president, the cabinet as a governmental institution is not very important.

However, the importance or unimportance of an institution is somewhat irrelevant compared to what we can learn by studying that institution. When reflected upon, the cabinet raises a number of questions without easy answers. For instance, if it is so unimportant, why have so many distinguished and important people served in it? One may answer that service depends upon the importance of the particular department that the secretary heads and proceed to cite names from the illustrious group of men who have headed the State Department, for instance. But one still has to confront the fact that talented, ambitious, and important people have served as secretaries to the "lesser" departments too. Why?

Another question without easy answer is, If the cabinet as a body is so unimportant, why do presidents invest so much time in building their cabinets? The cabinet must have some intrinsic value to presidents.

One reason why these questions are so difficult to answer is that our view of the cabinet, and other political bodies for that matter, has relied so heavily on sociological definitions of institutions. The most important statements about institutions and institutionalization in political science come from Nelson Polsby (1968) and Samuel Huntington (1968). Their statements derive heavily from the sociological perspective, especially the one taken by Max Weber and his heirs. That tradition stresses the capabilities of organizations as institutions. The sociological tradition concerns institutions in general. However, there are many types, or species, of organization. The species that most concerns political scientists is the political one. While the sociological tradition helps us understand organizations and institutions generally, it is too blunt to help us understand specific types of organization and institution.

Specifically, political institutions in a democracy may possess characteristics that undermine their institutional capabilities. These characteristics may be traced to the need to be representative. We have misunderstood the cabinet in part because we have relied upon a theory of institutions that emphasizes institutional capability. What is required, however, is a theory of democratic institutions, a theory that emphasizes the balance between the dual nature of representative government, that is, its need and capacity to act and also its ability to represent. The cabinet is important because of its representative qualities.

This is a somewhat ironic idea. The theory of government that led to the idea of separate branches—the legislative, the executive, and the judicial—placed responsibility for representing more with the legislative than the executive, while the executive was given more of the responsibility for action. Ironically, the cabinet, a part of the executive, is more of a representative body than one that has the capacity for action. This irony results in part from its political nature. Politicians, not bureaucrats, sit in the cabinet. It represents the party in power more than the career bureaucracy. And, most importantly, it has no corporate responsibility or authority.

This book is a study of the cabinet as a democratic institution and looks at both institutional capability and representativeness. In so doing, I will use traditional methods of analysis, especially when looking at institutional capability. In contrast, the question of representativeness will be addressed with quantitative materials when appropriate. The quantitative data are primarily about the secretaries, their careers, their characteristics, their political loyalties and ties. The use of quantitative data to study the cabinet is another innovation offered in this book. Not only have quantitative data been used rarely to study the cabinet (it has been studied so seldom), but much of the study of the executive, especially the presidency, has seemed to withstand the tide of behavioralism, quantification, systematic inquiry, and hypothesis testing that has swept so much of the rest of the discipline.

The last major charge of this book is to clarify some issues relating to representation theory. That theory has been applied mostly to legislative settings, with much success. However, the concept of representation has rarely been applied to the executive. This means that I will have to develop a vocabulary that may differ somewhat from what is found in legislative studies. Some issues of representation important to legislatures are unimportant to the executive, and the reverse is also true. For instance, constituency as an electorate takes on little importance for the cabinet, though the symbolic value of the secretary acting as a representative of a constituency may be important.

The work of Pitkin (1967), Eulau and Karps (1978), and Fenno (1978) provides the intellectual foundation for my discussion of representation. As I conceptualize the problem, representation is a dynamic relationship between representative and represented, and influence may flow in either direction. Hence, responsiveness is a crucial element of any true representative relationship. Here the secretary is defined as the representative; however, the definition of who is being represented cannot be set firm. This is because secretaries represent more than one interest. For example, do they represent the president in the bureaucracy or the interests of the bureaucracy at the White House? Who and what are the interests of a secretary's department? The answers to these questions change as the substantive problem and the context change.

Eulau and Karps (1978) suggest four types of representation based upon the target of the representative. These types are policy responsiveness, service responsiveness, allocative responsiveness, and symbolic responsiveness. As the introduction to chapter 3 details, only policy and symbolic responsiveness are relevant to the cabinet case, and my data speak more clearly and directly to symbolic and less well to policy responsiveness.

To recapitulate, three themes motivate this study. First, it clarifies our understanding of the cabinet. This is done by focusing on two important characteristics of representative governments: their ability to act, and their representativeness. Second, novel quantitative data on secretaries are brought to bear on these questions. Third, the concept of representation as it may apply to the executive branch of government is developed.

This book is divided into six chapters. The first two look at the cabinet as an institution. Chapter 1 discusses the place of the cabinet in the U.S. political system and the way in which it relates to political forces other than the president. These include the Congress, interest groups, and the bureaucracy.

Chapter 2 discusses the institutional cabinet. Institutionalization theory is applied to the cabinet case, and, not unexpectedly, I show that the cabinet is not very well institutionalized. Rather, it seems more personalized around the needs and desires of the president.

These needs and desires are important in understanding the political role of the cabinet, its representative role. This theme is developed in chapters 3–6.

Chapter 3 begins by inspecting the backgrounds of cabinet members. Four background characteristics are discussed using the quantitative career data: age, education, region, and occupation. A case is made for the cabinet's ability to be responsive both symbolically and with regard to policy.

Chapter 4 inspects the linkage of the cabinet to the party system. Parties are important institutions in helping to build governmental responsiveness. Strong ties between the cabinet and the parties are found, but they are also found to be time specific. The tension between the secretary's tendency to be more responsive to special interests than to political parties is also discussed in this chapter.

Chapter 5 looks at the way in which the informal hierarchy of departments, also called the inner-outer cabinet distinction, affects the policy responsiveness of the cabinet. In general, the background and career data collected for this study confirm the idea of department distinctiveness. However, the data also point to refinement of the distinction by suggesting a further one between the older departments of the outer cabinet and the newer ones.

The final substantive chapter, chapter 6, raises the question of the types of factor that may affect the length of tenure of the secretaries. Whereas most of the literature on high-level bureaucrats suggests that personal motivations are the key to government service, the data on secretaries hint that policy may also play a role. Tenure may be shortened or lengthened in part because of the success or failure of presidential policies. This pattern suggests another level of policy responsiveness by the cabinet.

The conclusion gives a brief summary of the findings. The lack of institutional capacity of the cabinet is contrasted with its representative character. Finally, I discuss a theory of modern democracy whereby democracy must be both capable and responsive. An institutional division of labor ensures the government's ability to do both simultaneously. The cabinet is related to this theory. From this we are able to understand the role of the cabinet in government in the United States.

★ 1 ★

The Cabinet in the

U.S. Political System

The cabinet occupies an ambiguous and complex position in the system of government of the United States. This ambiguity and complexity derive from the lack of constitutional provision for a cabinet, the separation of powers doctrine, and vagueness about the extent and limitations of presidential power and authority.

Though the Constitution does not provide for a cabinet, George Washington proceeded to build one early in his administration (McDonald 1974; Hoxie 1984). His initial cabinet officials included Thomas Jefferson at State, Henry Knox at the War Department, and Alexander Hamilton at Treasury. Soon afterward, the Attorney General's Office and the Post Office were organized, with Edmund Randolph and Samuel Osgood, respectively, heading those departments.

There was little initial objection to a cabinet, though the role that it was to play caused considerable discussion. Little objection to the cabinet arose because of (1) a historic familiarity with the idea of a cabinet (Fenno 1959, 9–20) and (2) the constitutional provisions that the president shall faithfully execute the laws and "may require the opinion, in writing, of the principal Officer in each of the executive Departments, upon any Subject relating to the Duties of their respective Offices" (Article II, Section 2, Clause 1).

Also, historic familiarity with cabinets, especially the British one, led many to believe that some type of cabinet was necessary (Hoxie 1984, 209–10; Fenno 1959, 12–16; McDonald 1974, 36–42; Horn 1960, 6–7; Laski 1940, 96–110). Key questions did arise, though: Whose cabinet, and what should be the relationship between the cabinet and the Congress (Horn 1960, 7–13). These early debates over cabinet-Congress relations were often voiced in terms of the boundaries between the president and Congress, and they reveal the complexity of the cabinet's political role in the U.S. government. This leads to the proposition that, though the ties between the cabinet and the president are clearly the most important, the cabinet also has significant relations with other actors in the political system, including the Congress, the departments, and interest groups. Though the focus of this book is on cabinet-president relations, to appreciate these fully, one must also understand the nature and strength of ties to the other political institutions and actors.

The Cabinet and Congress

The separation of powers structure of the federal government is the single most important descriptive fact about the U.S. political system and the reason it operates and behaves the way it does. Separation of powers should not be read too strictly, though. Abstractly, one may be able to distinguish legislative duties from executive ones from judicial ones, but practically there are many gray areas. Is appropriating money purely legislative, or are there not also executive properties in this action as well? The checks and balances written into the basic structure of the separation of powers reveal the overlap and sometimes meshing of the different government functions. And one therefore sees a picture of the federal system as one, to quote Neustadt's famous phrase, of "separated institutions, sharing powers" (1960, 33). Authority is separated, but power is shared.

The fact that the legislature sometimes exerts what would be considered executive powers opens up channels whereby the legislative branch may affect the cabinet. Cabinet relations with the Congress can be understood by looking at four issues: appointment; removal and impeachment; cabinet officers sitting in Congress, and cabinet lobbying in Congress.

Appointment

There are both formal and informal aspects of the Congress's role in the appointment of cabinet officers. The formal aspect of the relationship derives from the constitutional requirement of Senate confirmation of the president's nominee for the cabinet post by a margin of two-thirds plus one. Also, formal aspects of the relationship can be seen in the need to hold confirmation hearings.

The informal aspects of the cabinet-Congress relationship in the appointment process grows out of the formal. First, there is a general norm that the president should get the cabinet that he wants. However, that norm, as Mackenzie argues, is not "sacrosanct" (1981, 169). There have been instances when the Congress refused to confirm a presidential nominee. One example, with almost comic overtones, was that of Caleb Cushing, who was nominated by John Tyler for the post of treasury secretary three times on the same day in 1843 and rejected all three times.[1] A second example is the case of Lewis Strauss in 1958, whom the Senate refused to confirm as commerce secretary, ostensibly because, during a previous tenure as chairman of the Atomic Energy Commission, he refused to respond to the Joint Atomic Energy Committee's requests for information (Mackenzie 1981, 143).[2] There have also been some cases in which presidents withdrew names before the confirmation vote because of the likelihood of defeat and/or the degree of conflict that the nomination generated. In all, Mackenzie counts eight cases of Senate refusal to confirm a cabinet nominee since the beginning of the Republic (p. 170, n. 18).

A number of factors enter into the Senate's refusal to confirm a cabinet nominee. These relate to the goals that the members of the Senate pursue through the confirmation process. Mackenzie's study is much broader than the present one because he focuses on all major appointments to the executive branch, including under secretaries, independent regulatory commissioners, and other major executive appointments subject to senatorial confirmation. Still, his study can be useful in trying to understand the conditions under which the Senate is likely to refuse confirmation, even though there is a strong norm to give the president the cabinet that he wants.

Mackenzie lists a number of reasons why the Senate would not confirm a nominee: policy differences, conflict of interest, personal integrity, and the like (1981, 177–78; see also Riddlesperger 1986). Some of these issues have emerged in the recent nomination of Edwin Meese to the attorney general's post. Using roll call data, Mackenzie unearths some political motivations regarding Senate refusal to confirm. Though most such refusals are made by not taking any action, there are some confirmation votes in which the nominee received less than 100 percent. Mackenzie finds that about three-fourths of the votes against confirmation came from the opposition party. Those of the president's party who opposed the nomination were usually in philosophic or ideological disagreement with the president. For instance, during the Kennedy-Johnson years there was a strong relationship between support for the conservative coalition among Democrats and propensity to vote against the president's nominee (pp. 178–79).

Though refusing to confirm is rare and is usually motivated by a mixture of policy differences and partisan conflict, the appointment process in the Senate serves other important purposes. The confirmation hearings and investigations inform the Senate as to the nominee's personal qualities, character and integrity, competence for the position, and any possible conflict of interest. Further, the Senate uses the hearings to represent and advocate the interests of the senators' constituents. But most importantly, the hearings are used to affect public policy. The senators want to exchange views with the nominee about issues vital to the post, they want to gather information about the department as part of the Senate's oversight duties and functions, and, perhaps most crucially, they want the secretary designate to understand the Senate's position on issues relevant to the department (Mackenzie 1981, 97–173). In this sense one gets a taste of congressional-presidential conflict over control of the executive and the bureaucracy. Though the president may be constitutionally sanctioned to carry out the laws, the Congress is interested in ensuring that it is the Congress's policies that are implemented. Through these hearings, then, the Senate tries to inform cabinet officers that they have at least two masters, Congress as well as president.

Removal and Impeachment

Though Congress is constitutionally involved in the appointment process, its role in removing cabinet members from office is not so clearly spelled out. The greater the power and authority that Congress has over removing sitting cabinet officers, the more control it will have over the activities, behaviors, and policies pursued by the secretaries while in office. Two routes have been open to Congress to control the composition of the cabinet once formed; impeachment, which is difficult and restrictive; and the removal power, which limits the president's ability to remove cabinet members from office unilaterally and without Senate consent. Whereas the impeachment power is clearly granted to Congress,[3] the removal power is ambiguous.

Congress has only sparingly used the impeachment power. Only one cabinet officer has been impeached, but he was not convicted. Impeachment proceedings were called for in two other cases. William W. Belknap, secretary of war, was impeached in 1876 on the charge that he accepted "money for appointing and continuing in office a post trader at Fort Sill, Oklahoma" (Congressional Quarterly 1976, 143). Belknap's impeachment proceedings were part of general investigations of corruption in the administration. He was subsequently acquitted, though he resigned from office as a result of the impeachment.

Proceedings were commenced against two other secretaries but were dropped before the trial or conviction vote. Attorney General Harry M. Daughtery was implicated in the Teapot Dome scandal of 1922, and calls for impeachment were incited by his lack of action on the scandal. In due course, President Coolidge forced him to resign, and the proceedings ceased. The other case involved Herbert Hoover's treasury secretary, Andrew Mellon. Congressman Wright Patman of Texas called for Mellon's impeachment because of conflict of interest. Hoover was able to kill the impeachment by nominating Mellon to be ambassador to Great Britain, for which he was confirmed (Congressional Quarterly 1976, 138–39).

The great difficulties of congressional use of impeachment are its restrictions and the cumbersomeness of the procedure. The procedure involves both chambers, the House investigating and the Senate acting as a court. Further, massive majorities are needed to convict (two-thirds plus one), which is a very difficult hurdle to overcome in order to use impeachment as an effective instrument of personnel control. In fact, of the fourteen impeachment proceedings to reach the Senate, only five ended in conviction. (Eleven of the fourteen trials and all five convictions were of judges [Congressional Quarterly 1976, 127], which does not include Harry Claiborne's conviction in 1986). The restrictiveness revolves around the question of what constitutes an impeachable offense, with terms like *treason* and *high crimes and misdemeanors* leading many to argue that impeachment is permissible only for indictable offenses and not for policy reasons. Though the vague wording of the clause does not seem to prohibit policy as a reason to impeach (see Fisher 1978, 151), the fact that Congress has not seen fit to use it as a reason has probably foreclosed impeachment as a method of policy control, except in the most extraordinary of circumstances (Congressional Quarterly 1976, 135–37; Fisher 1978, 150–54).

The impeachment power is essentially a negative one. In contrast, the removal power has positive implications for Congress. In essence, the removal power gives Congress a role in removing officials from office. It historically has meant that, before a president could fire one of his secretaries, the removal action had to be approved (or at least not prohibited) by Congress. Thus, the positive aspect of cabinet control for Congress arises when, if a secretary disobeys the president and sides with Congress when policy disputes arise, Congress will not allow the president to remove the secretary from office.

The removal power has always been embroiled in controversy, and presidential-congressional conflict over it has led to one of the greatest constitutional crises the nation ever witnessed, the impeachment of Andrew Johnson. Fisher (1978) has identified a number of schools of thought concerning removal. First is the school that states that the Senate must have equal participation with the president in removing officers. This is justified in part by the Senate's role in confirmation. Second is an opposed line of thinking that argues that congressional involvement in removal can be made only through the constitutional route of impeachment. Third is a mode of logic that argues that, since Congress creates the executive departments (they were not created by the Constitution), Congress may attach conditions for tenure and removal. Fourth is a presidential supremacy argument, which posits that the power of removal is exclusively the duty of the president and that it derives as an incident of executive power (pp. 50–51).

Early on, during the debates over the creation of the first executive departments, a modified version of Madison's view of presidential power, which vested in the president the power to remove the secretaries of state, war, and treasury, carried the day (Fisher 1978, 51–56; Horn 1960, 7–10; Congressional Quarterly 1976, 230–31), though, as Fisher notes, "Congress did not intend to vest the entire removal power with" the president (p. 56). For example, when attention turned to the comptroller of the treasury, Madison, the presidentialist, argued that it was necessary to consider the nature of the office, and for an office not purely executive in nature "there may be strong reasons why an officer of this kind should not hold his office at the pleasure of the executive branch of the Government" (cited in Fisher 1978, 56). Still, these initial decisions gave the president, rather than Congress, personnel control of the cabinet.

The removal debates recurred in 1833, during Andrew Jackson's tenure. That the debate did not surface during the forty-year period prior to Jackson's administration is in part a function of the "great restraint" exercised by presidents in the interim years (Congressional Quarterly 1976, 231).

Unlike his predecessors, Jackson used the removal power as a partisan instrument. The spoils system is credited to Jackson and Van Buren, and removing officials from office is an effective way to create more patronage positions, which then may be dispensed. In fact, according to Fisher, Jackson used the power 252 times, compared to 193 for all of his predecessors (1978, 57). The removal power, though, was aimed during this period more at subcabinet- than cabinet-level posts, until Jackson removed his secretary of the treasury for not carrying out his policies concerning the Second United States Bank. The Senate subsequently censured Jackson but removed the censure three years later (Fisher 1978, 56—58; Congressional Quarterly 1976, 231—32; Horn 1960, 32—34).

It was during the administration of Andrew Johnson that all of the implications of a president and Congress at odds over removal were fully played out. Tension was high between Johnson and Congress because of a dispute over Reconstruction policy. Johnson favored Lincoln's reconciliation approach, but congressional Republicans, dominated by the radical faction, held a harder line. It was in this atmosphere that Congress passed the Tenure of Office Act in 1867. The act specified that a president could not remove an officer until he named a replacement with the advice and consent of the Senate. In other words, if the Senate refused to confirm a replacement, the original appointee would remain in office. Viewing the act not only as a severe abridgment of presidential authority, but also as a congressional encroachment on the executive branch, Johnson vetoed the bill, only to have his veto overridden. When Johnson tried to remove the secretary of war, Edwin Stanton, from office, Congress reacted, after considerable maneuvering, with impeachment proceedings (for concise descriptions of the issues involved see Fisher 1978, 58—59 and Congressional Quarterly 1976, pp. 232—33).

All presidents subsequent to Johnson called for repeal of the act. Finally, after twenty years it was repealed in 1887. Repealing the act also closed the book on presidential authority to remove cabinet officials. It was to be allowed without congressional interference. The cabinet had become the president's, though presidential power to remove other appointees is not so broad (Fisher 1978, 59—60, 80—81; Horn 1960, 74—77; Congressional Quarterly 1976, 233—34). As the issues of appointment and removal have evolved, congressional influence over the cabinet has been limited to the confirmation of nominees, but, as this review has argued, congressional input through the confirmation process is significant in creating ties and understandings between the cabinet and Congress.

Cabinet Officers in Congress?

Right after the creation of the initial cabinet offices, the issue of congressional relations with cabinet officers was raised. The Constitution had partially settled the question by prohibiting anyone from serving simultaneously in more than one branch of government. Therefore, the president could not create a cabinet from sitting members in Congress and build a quasi-parliamentary governmental system. Yet congressional concern for policy and the constitutional power to investigate the executive led some early members of Congress to institute a formal, if passive, relationship between the cabinet and Congress. Two variations on a theme were most often raised: (1) allowing cabinet officers to sit in Congress during debates and allowing them to debate (or at least speak) but not vote; and (2) presenting cabinet officers before Congress for question periods similar to those in the British Parliament. (Horn 1960, 10–16).

Horn has succinctly distilled the many positions on the debate. They basically come down to three points. First, those favoring participation in Congress by cabinet members have viewed policy making as being determined greatly by small groups of individuals, usually in committees. Bringing secretaries into active participation in Congress would open up the process. Second, another group of proponents felt that question periods would provide unity in the executive branch because, prior to congressional interrogation, a presidential position would have to be established and communicated unambiguously to the secretary. Third, on the opposing side was the view that cabinet officers would become disloyal or alienated from the president by trying to ingratiate themselves with Congress. Cabinet participation in Congress would thus lead to a weakening of executive coherence and congressional dominance of the departments (Horn 1960, 2–3).

Though the idea has been given serious consideration, including numerous bills and congressional debates, the opponents of cabinet participation have always carried the day. The issue now seems dead, though it was only forty years ago that Estes Kefauver proposed some type of cabinet question period (Horn 1960, 137–75). Of some related interest are results of a survey of Congress that Horn conducted showing a desire on the part of Congress to establish better relations with the cabinet but a lack of enthusiasm for a formal relationship of the question period type (pp. 199–210).

Cabinet Officers as Lobbyists

The above sections have underscored the limited formal ties between the cabinet and Congress, of which appointment is the only one of significance for their ongoing interaction. Though formal linkages may be limited, informal ones do exist. Most importantly, the secretary is an envoy from the administration to Congress and engages in what one could term executive lobbying of Congress.

Cabinet lobbying or informal interaction with Congress takes a number of forms. Fenno (1959, 199–204) reviewed these most clearly over twenty years ago, and his analysis is still pertinent today. Most obviously, the president may use the secretary to sell the president's program to Congress. Less obvious, but still important, is that the secretary, through interacting with the Congress, may be able to gather important information about congressional preferences, which may be useful in developing presidential legislative strategies. Further, as Greenstein (1982) illustrates, the secretary may be used to deflect criticism from the president. Also of significance, presidents may use secretaries when launching legislative trial balloons. If the proposal does not fly, the president may be insulated from criticism by not publicly favoring the policy. In each of these ways, informal relations of secretaries with Congress may be of use to the president.

The Secretary and the Department

The secretary stands not only between the president ·and Congress, feeling tugs of varying strength from both, but also between the president and the department's bureaucracy. This position is most fundamental for the cabinet officer, for it poses a paradox: the secretary is to be the president's advocate in the depths of the department's bureaus, and, to be an effective advocate, must be a strong secretary. Yet to be able to influence the department, the cabinet member must also be a strong advocate for the department in the White House. A secretary perceived by the department as not vigorously pursuing its interests will surely not find as much cooperation as one who is perceived as acting in pursuit of its interests.

The role of the secretary as presidential advocate looms more important when one looks closely at the centrality to the president of management of the bureaucracy and its programs. A president, in order to be effective, must be certain that presidential policies have been implemented. But, as numerous studies have shown, there are bureaucratic structures and decision-making routines that may frustrate presidential control. For instance, Aberbach and Rockman (1976) emphasize the impact of party, ideology, and bureau socialization patterns on the behaviors of bureaucrats (see also Cronin 1980 and Cole and Caputo 1979 on these points). Also, the long tenure and incremental decision routines of bureaucrats may inhibit presidential attempts at control. In an important specification of this theory, Randall (1979) shows that presidents can affect and direct the bureaucracy, but only if they are willing to invest the energy and time. No president has the time to expend on every agency or program, and the secretary is therefore all the more important to the president. This point may be underscored by the fact that presidents place a high premium on managerial ability when naming replacement cabinet officers (Polsby 1978; Best 1981; King and Riddlesperger 1984).

Secretaries may find important constraints on control of their departments beyond the issue of divided loyalty that opened this section. In a study of the Department of Health, Education, and Welfare, Greenberg identified a number of important limitations to secretarial control (1980). Though his findings are based on the agency that is probably the most difficult to manage, Greenberg's general points are well taken for most of the cabinet-level departments (and other administrative agencies as well).

First of all, a secretary's management of a department may be impeded if the department is not focused on a clear goal or set of goals, and if definition of those goals is not easy. Such a problem will plague most of the multipurpose departments (and may be one of the major defects of Nixon's supercabinet proposal, which he suggested would facilitate management). Second, lack of discretion may impede the president's control through the secretary. Lack of discretion usually is a result of congressional statute writing and can be seen in such examples as categorical versus block grants, congressional and legislative vetoes, and rules over administrative rule making, to cite only some of the more obvious forms. Lastly, departments filled with professionally oriented personnel may resist both president and secretary as the bureaucrats maintain loyalty to their profession, not their administration. Classic examples may be the social workers at the Department of Health and Human Services, environmentalists at the Environmental Protection Agency, or scientists at the Department of Energy (Greenberg 1980).

Still, this is not to say that secretaries are helpless in the face of their departments. There is much that a secretary can do, especially if supported by a popular president who is concerned about policy, but the job of department management is likely to be one of the most trying, complex, and difficult jobs for the secretary.

The Secretary and Interest Groups

Just as cabinet officers have relationships with the Congress and with their own departments, so also do they interact and communicate with interest groups. Strong interest group relationships are not constant across departments, though. Some secretaries have strong ties to strong interests, whereas for others interests are only a weak or even a nonexistent factor. This variability comes about from the conditions that motivated the creation of the department. Some departments, such as Agriculture, Interior, Labor, and Education, were created because of political pressures exerted by interests. Others, such as State, were created for other reasons, for instance to perform a necessary governmental duty (Fenno 1959, 9–20). The more important the interest in the creation of the department, the more important the interest will probably be as a constraint (or asset) for the secretary.

The creation of the cabinet departments seems to have occurred in waves or clusters, and this temporal pattern is consistent with patterns that modernization and development theory would posit. The first wave swiftly ushered in six departments in a nine-year period (1789–

98). The six early departments were, in order, those of State, War, Treasury, the Attorney General, the Postmaster General, and the Navy. All of these can be said to perform vital government functions, for example, developing relations with other nations, defending the nation, regulating the currency, implementing the laws, and delivering the mail. These are functions that no government, however limited, can avoid.

The next wave, which occurred over a longer time, can be termed the interest group wave. These departments were created because of the demands of important sectors in the economy (Interior in 1849, Agriculture in 1889, Commerce and Labor in 1903, which was divided into separate departments in 1913). Generally, these departments are considered to be the ones most likely to be dominated by a strong interest group, and they are also the ones for which secretaries are most likely to appear as interest group advocates. Further, the importance of the interest to the department has often given the interest an important role in determining the secretary, such that the secretary of labor would have to be acceptable to labor, the secretary of agriculture acceptable to farm interests, and so on.

The last wave, which began in 1953, can be said to be that of departments fostering the interests of broad classes of people, especially the disadvantaged and consumers. Often these departments are characterized by numerous interest group clients, sometimes in conflict, but usually lacking in the political power and resources of the economic interests of the second-wave departments. Rather than being the captive of the interests, department secretaries of the third wave must often negotiate and find balances and compromises among the competing interests. It was for just these reasons that educational interests pushed for a separate cabinet department, which was organized in 1979 (Miles 1978).

Many scholars have argued that cabinet members are more likely to be interest group advocates than presidential advocates. This view is too simplistic. First of all, not all departments have environments where interests groups are important. Second, even for departments where single interests are dominant (those in the second wave), the interest may be a vital element of the coalition of groups in the president's party, and therefore it may be more likely to agree with presidential policy than disagree with it (Wilson 1977). Lastly, at least for the departments with competing interests, secretaries may be able to position themselves in such a way that they can side with the president by brokering between the competing interests. When it is not possible to stay out of the interest group fray, the secretary can still side with the interest that is closer to the president's position. The main impact of interests on cabinet-president relations is not that they will always exert pressure on the secretary to oppose presidential policy, but that, at the collective cabinet level, the many interests represented by the different departments will vie for priority status within the president's program.

Conclusion

Secretaries are not only responsible to the president. They must also take into account the demands of the Congress, interest groups, and their own departments. Noting the multiplicity of demands on cabinet officers does not make them unique in U.S. politics: most actors in the system are in similar positions.

However, these competing demands do limit how much the president can rely on and use the cabinet. Not only do they frustrate the cabinet's collective responsibility and behavior, which limits its utility for the president, but also they limit the value of individual secretaries to the president. The next chapter will discuss these limitations as they relate to the collective cabinet. Succeeding chapters will focus on limitations on the president's ability to rely on individual secretaries.

★ 2 ★

The Institutionalization

of the Cabinet

In his seminal study, Fenno (1959) opened up the question of the institutionalization of the cabinet. Reading Fenno's documentation of the institutional enhancements provided to the cabinet during the Eisenhower years, one comes away from the analysis with a positive feeling about the institutional development of that body. However, because Fenno's analysis ended before the accession of the Kennedy administration, he was unable to witness and take into account the rapid and extreme deinstitutionalization of the cabinet by Kennedy. Unrecognized by Fenno was the fact that Eisenhower's institutional enhancement of the cabinet was prompted by his personal preferences. And personal preferences led to Kennedy's institutional dismantling of the cabinet.

This historical review raises a number of important questions. First, why was Kennedy able to deinstitutionalize the cabinet but unable to dispense with it totally? How is such an institutionally weak body as the cabinet able to resist these attacks on it? Second, are there forces aside from presidential preferences that may promote a more institutionally secure cabinet? Third, what is the utility of institutionalization theory in understanding the role of the cabinet in politics in the United States?

These questions are linked, and I will try to make the following points in this chapter. First, institutionalization theory is highly limited in explaining the historic longevity but institutional anemia of the cabinet. This is due in part to the sociological focus of the theory. It is erroneous to think of the cabinet as a formally integrated institution. Rather, it is more a collection of a dozen or so secretaries who sometimes meet together in sessions called by the president, and at his whim.

Second, there are environmental forces, notably the interaction of the size of government and the need to control government policy, that may enhance the institutional capability of the cabinet. This will be done more by integrating the cabinet with the policy-making organs of the White House Office and Executive Office of the President than by converting it into a full-fledged institution.

This chapter begins by reviewing institutionalization theory. The theory is then applied to the cabinet case. The concluding section discusses the limits of that theory. Succeeding chapters develop an alternative theory for understanding the cabinet, one that emphasizes its representational qualities.

Defining Institutionalization

Extensive literature exists on the institutionalization processes within the executive branch, especially the Executive Office of the President and the White House Office (Greenstein 1979; Seligman 1956; Neustadt 1954, 1955; Gilmour 1975; Light 1983; Wyszomirski 1982), and with some limited reference to the cabinet (Fenno 1959). The cabinet has seen ups and downs in its institutional development. The high point may have been the Eisenhower years, but the Reagan administration has made major efforts to improve the institutional capacity of the cabinet. To understand the nature of the cabinet's institutional development and the causes of the deinstitutionalization of the Eisenhower cabinet system under Kennedy, one needs a theoretical guide and not just a historical account. Institutionalization theory, based on the major conceptual work of Huntington (1968, 1973), Polsby (1968), Kesselman (1970), and Gilmour (1975), will serve as that guide. This section begins by reviewing some of the literature on institutionalization. The remainder of the chapter applies the concept to the cabinet.

Two works stand out in clarifying and directing research on the concept of institutionalization: Samuel Huntington's *Political Order in Changing Societies* (1968) and Nelson Polsby's paper, "The Institutionalization of the U.S. House of Representatives" (1968).

Polsby defines an institutionalized organization as having

> three major characteristics: 1) it is relatively well bounded, that is to say, differentiated from its environment. Its members are easily identifiable, it is relatively difficult to become a member, and its leaders are recruited principally from within the organization. 2) The organization is relatively complex, that is, its functions are internally separated on some regular and explicit basis, its parts are not wholly interchangeable, and for at least some important purposes, its parts are interdependent. There is a division of labor in which roles are specified, and there are widely shared expectations about the performance of roles. There are regularized patterns of recruitment to roles, and of movement from role to role. 3) Finally, the organization tends to use universalistic rather than particularistic criteria, and automatic, rather than discretionary methods for conducting its internal business. Precedents and rules are followed; merit systems replace favoritism and nepotism; and impersonal codes supplant personal preferences as prescriptions for behavior.

Thus Polsby identifies three important components of institutions: boundaries, complexity, and universalism. Huntington (1968, 1973), who also has much to say about the concept, does not offer exactly the same criteria for defining an institution. Huntington offers four important characteristics: autonomy, complexity, adaptability, and coherence. Though there is some overlap with Polsby (both identify complexity in roughly the same way), there are some notable differences, though these are not exclusive.

For instance, autonomy is not quite the same thing as boundedness. Both focus on separation from the environment of the institution, but boundedness relies more heavily on internal career paths than does autonomy. Autonomy is somewhat broader and also looks at where decisions affecting the institution are made.

Further, Huntington and Polsby seem to differ on whether or not institutionalization is a unified process. Polsby seems to indicate that institutions may develop the different characteristics at different rates. Huntington tends to view the process as more unified; the different aspects of institutionalization develop at similar speeds and in tandem. In an important theoretical refinement, Kesselman (1970) points out that some aspects of institutionalization may impede the development of other aspects. For instance, well-secured boundaries may limit or inhibit an institution's adaptive capacity. Similarly, extreme internal complexity may lead to institutional incoherence rather than coherence.

From the literature, one can construct a set of characteristics that is relevant to the institutional development of the cabinet. The set includes autonomy-boundedness, complexity, coherence, and adaptability. These will be used to measure the degree of institutionalization of the cabinet, trace the history of its institutional development, and point the directions in which it seems to be moving. Special note will be made of Reagan's reforms, especially the cabinet council system. These characteristics will also help to judge some important reform proposals and attempts in recent years.

Autonomy and Boundedness

The cabinet is by no means autonomous though it posseses some important, but limited, boundaries from its environment. Its key boundary is that its members can be identified (though if one takes a more functional approach, the existence of kitchen cabinets surely obscures matters). Legal statutes creating the several departments identify cabinet officials (it is assumed that department chiefs will be cabinet members), and in 1907 the first statutory reference to the cabinet was made. The act related to salary increases, and the reference reads, "the heads of executive departments who are members of the President's Cabinet" (cited in Hoxie 1984, 221).

However, identification of cabinet members is far from unambiguous. For instance, not all cabinet members are departmental secretaries, the United Nations ambassador, the director of the Central Intelligence Agency, and the special trade representative being the three current examples. Also, the attendance of presidential aides at cabinet meetings further erodes the definitiveness of the cabinet's boundaries. Whether one defines the cabinet as those who attend its meetings or as those who head departments has implications for the discussion of cabinet boundedness. That there is no agreed-upon definition is important in itself and underlines the general noninstitutional character of the cabinet. For the sake of clarity, when I refer to the cabinet, I mean the heads of the executive departments.

But crucially, the cabinet is not autonomous because it is overly dependent on the president.[1] The president decides who will be the members of the cabinet and what role it will play in the administration. Unlike parliamentary systems, where cabinet and chief executive form a team and are indistinguishable, the U.S. cabinet is subservient to the president.

One can see this presidential dominance when disputes between the president and cabinet officers arise. For example, there is the famous story about Lincoln, who decided on a course of action, though his cabinet voted unanimously against it. Similarly, the president can seek the resignation of members of the cabinet with whom there is disagreement or an inability to work. One such example is the recent departure of Alexander Haig. Engaged in a major foreign policy dispute with President Reagan and other key Reagan advisors, Haig had to lose, and he did, and was forced to leave. Other examples of disputes between the president and cabinet officials may be found (see Weisband and Frank 1975), but they all point to the same conclusion: secretaries generally lose in disagreements with the president.[2]

Presidential dominance is not omnipotent, though, and other factors display further environmental constraints on the cabinet. First of all, presidents do not have complete latitude in whom they appoint. As Fenno (1959) and others point out, there must be geographic and interest representation to form a balanced cabinet. As such, labor expects a labor man at the Department of Labor, farmers want a farmer at

Agriculture, and so forth. Beyond these political factors that constrain the president's freedom of choice are Congress (see chapter 1) and its confirmation power.

Polsby cites a few factors to help identify the boundedness of an organization. One is the difficulty of membership, as compared to the controllability of membership. On one level it is difficult to become a member of the cabinet. Only 468 people, as of December 1984, have so served, but consider the many hundreds of millions of Americans who have lived during those two-hundred years. Further, as chapter 3 will detail greatly, there are high qualifications for the office, such as education, and skills. However, many people have declined the presidential invitation to serve, a fact that may indicate a limited desirability of a cabinet post (Fenno 1959, 68–77).

Also, there is the question of leadership. Can the cabinet select its own leaders? On a formal level this is a meaningless question. Unquestionably, the president is the leader of the cabinet, and there are no formal subleadership positions to which cabinet members may aspire. Informally, leaders may arise in the cabinet from its ranks because of force of personality, for instance (see Cronin 1980, 253–96), but this type of leadership is not what is meant by leadership in institutional theory. Distinctions among cabinet members due to differential department status may occur, for instance, the inner versus outer cabinet (Fenno 1959, 117–19; Cronin 1980, 274–86), but the inner-outer distinction refers to influence with the president, not necessarily leadership of the cabinet, and again, it is informal, and not rigidly or formally set down.

Only once, during Richard Nixon's administration, were status distinctions made among cabinet members. In early 1973, Nixon announced that four secretaries would not only keep their cabinet duties but would be given the added duty of counselors to the president (Nathan 1983, 51–52). These supersecretaries (Secretary of the Treasury George Shultz, Secretary of Agriculture Earl Butz, Secretary of Health, Education, and Welfare Caspar Weinberger, and Secretary of Housing and Urban Development James Lynn) would, in effect, have closer access to the president than other secretaries and would in some ways merge the role of presidential advisor, the role White House staff people play, with

that of secretary.[3] And not only would they serve as presidential counselors, but three would chair their respective areas on the Domestic Council
(Butz on natural resources, Weinberger on human resources, and Lynn
on community development) and all four would be in charge of certain
broad policy areas (Shultz, economic affairs; Butz, natural resources;
Weinberger, human resources; Lynn, community development) (see Nathan 1983, 51–52). However, Nixon's experiment in status distinctions
was not followed by subsequent presidents, perhaps because of Watergate and the need of his successors to distance themselves from any action
that smacked of Nixonism.

On a last level, one may ascertain an organization's boundaries by
looking at how it conducts business, whether it meets frequently and
regularly. It had become a custom for the cabinet to meet on Tuesdays
and Fridays (Fenno 1959, 92). Even such presidents as Lincoln and
Wilson, who did not rely on their cabinets much, still gave in and held
periodic meetings. However, holding regular meetings was not immu-
table for Kennedy did not hold frequent or regular meetings. He found
them a waste of time. "Cabinet meetings are simply useless. . . . I
don't know how Presidents functioned with them or relied upon them
in the past" (cited in Hoxie 1984, 224–25). Though custom had led to
periodic and regular cabinet meetings, custom was not strong enough
to institutionalize such regularity if a president with a strong enough
will and a strong enough desire to dispense with regular meetings did
so. Yet, however much Kennedy disliked cabinet meetings, and
though regular, predictable meetings were not held after the early
months of his administration, he was not able to dispense with them
completely—some still had to be held.

The cabinet fails to meet the more stringent tests of boundedness and
autonomy: membership control, leadership development, career building,[4] and periodicity and predictability of meeting. Further, on the
easier test of member identifiability, it does not clearly pass either.

Complexity

The cabinet has never been a very complex organization. It would be
hard for any organization of a dozen or so members to be very complex.

Yet its level of complexity has been increasing over the years. This is seen not only in the expansion in the number of departments, but also in Nixon's attempts to rationalize the cabinet and Reagan's elaboration of cabinet councils.

Polsby has remarked on the inappropriateness of a count of committees to measure congressional complexity. The same point holds for the cabinet. Counting the number of members will not adequately measure its complexity. Such a count has to contend not only with the creation of new departments but also with the consolidation of the navy and war departments into the Defense Department and the removal of the postmaster general from the cabinet by converting the Post Office into a government corporation.

Yet other data indicate a growing complexity in the cabinet. This is best understood by referring to the division of labor. Complexity inheres when an organization takes large and/or difficult tasks and breaks them into smaller, discrete units on which to work. Further, complexity proceeds when the organization assigns different people to different parts of the tasks at hand, continues these job distinctions over time, and promotes specialization in the organization's work force.

Presidents and others have remarked on the inefficiency of having the whole cabinet sit on problems that affect only one or a few departments. What role will the secretary of the interior play in discussions of foreign policy, or the secretary of state in matters of urban problems. A key problem of the cabinet has been the tension between appointing policy specialists to the body and expecting it to deal with problems at a general policy level.[5]

One solution to this problem that has been offered is to divide the cabinet into subunits, have only members with the relevant expertise and those departments affected by a problem meet, excluding the uninterested. Further, full cabinet meetings would be reserved for only the broadest and most general policy problems and for development of team support for the president's program and policies (see Hess 1976 on this last point). One can see the seeds of this argument taking root in specific councils of which secretaries are members, though nonsecretaries may also be members. Two venerable examples include the National Security Council and the Council on Wage and Price Stability. Some of the other noteworthy councils and cabinet subgroups since the end of World War II include the Defense Mobilization Board (an advisory body for the Office of Defense Mobilization), the Advisory Board on Economic Growth and Stability (an advisory board of the Council of Economic Advisors), the National Aeronautics and Space Council, the National Council on Marine Resources and Engineering Development, the Council on International Economic Policy, and the Energy Resources Council. And there have been instances of interdepartmental committees composed of subgroups of secretaries, such as the Committee on Water Resources and Transportation Policy under Eisenhower (Fenno 1959, 140), but for the most part, these committees have been ad hoc and of short duration.

The Nixon administration began some of the first major experiments with councils outside the national security realm, of which cabinet members would often be members. To the legally mandated National Security Council, which began in 1946, Nixon added the Domestic Council in 1970. The Domestic Council was not purely a cabinet council, though, for it was headed by John Ehrlichman, a White House staff advisor. Within the Domestic Council working groups were forged on problem areas, such as welfare reform. Again, the welfare reform working group was headed by a White House staffer (Edward Morgan), but representatives from the departments of Labor, Health, Education, and Welfare, and the Bureau of the Budget (later the Office of Management and Budget) also served on it. But while departments were represented on these councils, department secretaries rarely were involved directly. The linkage here was mostly between the White House and subcabinet officials, and this not only tended to push secretaries out of the picture but also increased tensions between the White House and the secretaries, and among the secretaries of the participating departments as well (Nathan 1983, 35; also Pfiffner 1986).

This movement has come to some kind of fruition under Ronald Reagan. Numerous cabinet councils were created by Reagan, seven in all (abbreviations and dates of creation are noted in parentheses): Economic Affairs (CCEA, February '81), Commerce and Trade (CCCT, February '81), Food and Agriculture (CCFA, February '81), Human Resources (CCHR, February '81), Natural Resources and Environment (CCNRE, February '81), Legal Policy (CCLP, January '82), and Management and Administration (CCMA, September '82). And these councils were very active during the first eighteen months of the Reagan administration—they acted upon some two hundred issues (Hoxie 1984, 226; also Newland 1983, 1985).

Nathan (1983) summarizes the Reagan cabinet council process well. "(T)he cabinet council's work is conducted in three phases. Issues begin at the lowest level. The staff secretariat, made up of representatives of each of the council members and chaired by staff from the Office of Policy Development, writes policy papers. Next, cabinet-level working sessions, chaired by the designated secretary, refine the issues" (p. 73). Finally, policy decisions are made in sessions sometimes chaired by the president (Newland 1983). Each council had a staff secretariat, which was composed of representatives from each member department but was to be headed by staff from the Office of Policy Development in the White House. At the secretarial level of the councils, Office of Management and Budget personnel were in attendance. Only at the highest-level meetings, when the president attended, did other White House people regularly attend (Nathan 1983, 72–73).

Early observers, such as Nathan, felt that the cabinet council system was a success: "On the whole, . . . the councils are active and do make many decisions" (1983, 73). And "the reason that they operate more effectively . . . traces to the appointment process and the fact that the officials in the Reagan administration have such a strong set of shared ideological positions" (p. 73).[6]

However, later observers, notably Newland, offer a less rosy picture of the success of the cabinet council system. Though it is true that the system has helped to build networks linking White House and cabinet personnel, the councils have been relegated mostly to secondary issues, presidential participation at the councils has been slight, and the councils' work has emphasized the details of agenda enforcement and implementation.

Newland (1983, 1985) reports data supporting the view of limited cabinet council success. First, Reagan attended only 14 percent of council meeting through June 1982 (Newland 1983, 9). Further, on only 15 percent of the decisions coming from the councils' meetings did Reagan make a decision either at the meeting or later by acting on a recommendation coming from a meeting (Newland 1983, 7). Lastly, by fall 1983, the cabinet council system was in relative disuse. Two of the councils were dormant (CCNRE, CCFA), two were marginally active (CCHR, CCLP), one was modestly active (CCCT), one was strongly active (CCMA), and one was extremely busy (CCEA) (Newland 1985, 14).

Though not a resounding success by these figure, if one uses the criterion of bringing the cabinet, through the councils, into the top level of presidential policy making, the councils were successful, at least as long as they were used, in integrating the White House and cabinet and helped ensure that departmental secretaries were exposed constantly to the president's larger policy views. This helped to mute departmentalism in Reagan's cabinet, which may be the first not plagued by this often persistent division. However, the general deactivation of the council system may indicate, again, that this reform did not reflect institutionalizing tendencies so much as personal presidential preferences.

Aside from organizational structure, complexity can be seen in the resources assigned to internal management, such as facilities, personnel, and money (Polsby 1968, 158). From very early days, the cabinet was assigned its own room, the Cabinet Room, which is just off of the president's main office, the Oval Office in the White House. Such a physical location, assigned only for cabinet meeting use, provided the cabinet with not only a sense of location but also a sense of prestige.

However, the cabinet has not received much in the way of institutional resources. It was not until the Eisenhower administration that it had any staff assigned to it in the office of the cabinet secretary. Under Eisenhower, the cabinet secretary was charged with preparing and circulating the agenda of the cabinet meeting and following up decisions made by the cabinet in session. Follow-up generally consisted of charting the progress of the department secretaries on policies decided upon during the cabinet meeting. Also, the cabinet secretary was instructed to take notes on the cabinet meeting, though complete minutes of these meetings have never been kept (Fenno 1959, 96–97; Greenstein 1982).

The cabinet secretary's office was short lived; Kennedy subsequently discontinued it. This action reflects Kennedy's lack of confidence in the cabinet. However, the cabinet secretary's office reappeared in the Ford administration and has been a mainstay since, for Ford and his successors, Carter and Reagan, believed in a stronger cabinet and attempted to shore it up as an organization. It is probably safe to say that the cabinet secretary will exist into the foreseeable future and may now be a permanent component of the cabinet.

Yet, one must not overlook the fact that the cabinet secretary's office is very small and has no powers over the department secretaries. This discussion of the cabinet secretary underscores the weakness of the institutional and personnel supports for the cabinet.

Institutional Coherence

Perhaps the greatest institutional weakness of the cabinet is its lack of coherence. Coherence refers to the ability of the parts of a body to work together, to act in the interests of the whole, while minimizing internal differences. In a sense, coherence gives an institution a sense of self. The cabinet has little sense of self—rather, it has many selves. This lack of institutional coherence is all the more striking because of the trade-off between coherence and complexity. According to Kesselman (1970) very complex bodies tend toward institutional incoherence, whereas less complex organizations are often more institutionally coherent. That the cabinet is not too complex should lead to a prediction of institutional coherence, but such is not the case.

Lack of cabinet coherence moves in two directions, though motivated from the same source, departmentalism. Departmentalism's two directions pit, first, department secretary against president, and second, secretary against secretary. Charles G. Dawes, an early director of the Bureau of the Budget, was once quoted as saying, "Every member of the Cabinet is a natural enemy of the President." Though this may be an overstatement of the relationship between the president and his cabinet appointees (see Wilson 1977 for more on this point), there are important sources of tension between presidents and secretaries.

These sources are quite well known. Presidents have an incentive to constrain budget growth. Secretaries, however, have an incentive to increase their department's budget and budgetary share. Presidents see their programs as having top priority, secretaries view their own departments as most important.[7] Nixon staffers complained of cabinet members "going native," that is, becoming spokespersons in the White House for the clients of the department rather than presidential advocates in the departments (see Nathan 1983; Aberbach and Rockman 1976).

These same forces drive secretaries apart. They compete with one another for presidential favor and priority status in the president's program and budget. At times their department's clientele groups may disagree and conflict. Thus, departmentalism, which is rooted in the plural nature of U.S. politics, helps to undermine the institutional coherence of the cabinet (Fenno [1959] also makes this point).

Departmentalism has long been noted by observers of the cabinet, but two factors may be weakening the hold of the departments and their interests on the secretaries. The first is what Polsby (1977, 1978; 1983, 89–105) sees as a trend away from selecting representatives of interests for the cabinet in favor of selecting experts or managers whose prime loyalty is to the president. One factor motivating this shift, according to Polsby, has been the reforms of the presidential nominating process, which have helped weaken the influence of established interests on the choice of the nominee, therefore allowing the president more latitude in the selection of cabinet members. However, one must remark that such a trend did not insulate Carter from disharmony with his cabinet nor dissuade him from his midterm sweep of his cabinet. Part of his motivation for removing Califano from Health, Education, and Welfare and Blumenthal from Treasury was their disagreement with Carter policy.

A second trend, which may be more important, is based on the size, scope, and complexity of the federal government and on budgetary pressures to contain, coordinate, and rationalize the parts to the whole. As the economic expansion of the 1950s and 1960s has slowed and the budget has become pinched by these pressures, the need to control and manage has become more important.

The first signs of this pressure were felt during the Nixon years.

Nixon's policy approach centered on administrative control rather than on trying to build support coalitions in Congress. The large numbers of liberal Democrats in Congress precluded effective legislative strategy on Nixon's part. His conservative goals were not likely to be received favorably there. Therefore, he shifted focus to administrative control of the bureaucracy. For such an approach to succeed, Nixon required an effective, loyal, and strong administration. This included the cabinet (Nathan 1983; Aberbach and Rockman 1976). Thus, one can view Nixon's promise of a greater role for the cabinet as being more than merely symbolic. The strong cabinet idea has its roots in his policy control strategy.

But to control the bureaucracy, Nixon would need not only strong secretaries, but also a cabinet that functioned as a group. The secretaries must view Nixon's large policy goals as their own, and they must be able to motivate their departments in that direction. Further, they must subordinate departmental concerns to presidential policy. Nixon's strategy thus entailed overcoming, to some degree, the strong elements of departmentalism that so characterized the cabinet and the departments. To do so, he sought to reorganize the cabinet along functional lines.

As an early step, Nixon announced, shortly before his second inaugural, that certain cabinet members would be upgraded and given the role of special counselor to the president—the supersecretaries, mentioned above. Thus, one sees Nixon not only trying to relate the departments to each other but also, through the Domestic Council, trying to relate policy implementation, traditionally located in the cabinet, with policy development, which has mostly been located in the White House (see also Price [1983] on this general point).

The Nixon reorganization attempts followed the Ash Council recommendations and were sent to Congress. If Congress had accepted the Nixon reforms, one would have witnessed an institutional reform of the cabinet that would have been passed on to future presidents, thereby giving it some permanence. The reorganization specifically called for the reorganization of seven departments into four superdepartments (Human Resources, Community Development, Natural Resources, and Economic Affairs). But the Congress refused to enact the proposals, in part because they would disrupt congressional committee jurisdictions and upset committee relations with the bureaucracy and the interests (Dodd and Schott 1979, 340–46; Seidman 1980, 110–24), and because of the often noted congressional suspicion of and antipathies toward Nixon (Fisher 1978).

Still, the Nixon proposals are important because they reflect not only a president's desire to control the bureaucracy but also the response of the federal government to budgetary constraint. Thus, some attempts at promoting cabinet coherence and overcoming departmental parochialism were bound to recur.

The Watergate scandals momentarily halted the impetus for reform, and the proposals were also plagued by the fear of investing too much power in the presidency, again a consequence of Watergate. Though both Ford and Carter called for greater cabinet importance, other than the creation of Education and Energy under Carter, there was little fundamental cabinet change during their administrations. It was not until the Reagan administration that the push for a more coherent and effective cabinet was tried again.

Remember, cabinet coherence is especially concerned with the relationship of the president to the secretaries and of the secretaries to one another. Reagan's cabinet strategy, somewhat like Nixon's, moved in both directions.

First, Reagan insisted upon a loyal cabinet and subcabinet, one that would be resistant to the pressures coming from departmental interests. One approach to insulating cabinet officers and other political appointees relied upon the appointment process.

As an initial move, cabinet appointees were taught about their departments not by departmental personnel but by conservative task forces. Further, to help foster secretarial ties to the White House, numerous cabinet meetings were held during the transition period with the president in attendance. According to Nathan, these meetings were held "more for indoctrination than to discuss policy issues or decide upon policy options" (1983, 75). This process, it was hoped, would develop strong vertical ties from the secretary to the White House (see also Walker and Reopel 1984, esp. pp. 13–23).

Horizontal ties among the secretaries were to be built through the use of the cabinet councils mentioned above. Though ties to the White House can be seen here, on the whole the Reagan administration has tried to preserve the distinction between policy making and policy implementation (Nathan 1983, 71). Heclo views this system with a slightly different emphasis that focuses on moves by the Reagan White House to centralize decision making there. This was further reinforced when the Domestic Council was given responsibility not only for coordinating the cabinet councils and interdepartmental issues but also for policy developed within single departments (Heclo 1983, 46–47). Both Heclo (1983, 47) and Nathan (1983, 73) suggest that the cabinet council system under Reagan was able to insulate "political executives from the permanent departmental bureaucracies and from congressional committees by continually convening the executives in meetings under White House auspices" (Heclo 1983, 47); but Nathan also cites the importance of ideological homogeneity produced through the appointment process (1983, 73; see also Newland [1983, 1985], who offers a more limited view of their success).

In the end, the disuse of the councils must mark their failure at trying to overcome cabinet incoherence permanently and institutionally. But the problem of cabinet coherence has been motivated by outside environmental forces, such as budgetary constraint, the size of the government, the complexity of government programs, and the like, all of which may fall under the rubric of the need to control the policy instruments of government, and thus attempts at developing a more coherent cabinet are likely to be made in the future. This point will be developed more fully in the concluding section.

Adaptability

Adaptability refers to the ability of an institution to respond to a changing environment. The cabinet has a complex environment that consists of Congress, interests, and the departments themselves, but the president clearly stands out as the key environmental influence.

In one sense the cabinet responds well to the rotation of presidents in office, but in another sense this just displays its inherent institutional weakness. For the most part, presidents can use the cabinet as they wish. Some rely on it, and other do not, and reliance may vary by issue within administrations. Though the ability of the cabinet to conform to presidential preferences has implications for its longevity, this adaptability (or perhaps more precisely, malleability) has also undermined its institutional integrity.

One can see this clearly by reflecting upon the development of the cabinet during the Eisenhower period and Kennedy's subsequent dismantling of those accoutrements of institutions. In a sense, Fenno is wrong about the institutional development of the cabinet during the Eisenhower years. The cabinet did not institutionalize, and resources vanished, because it was responding to the personal style of a president (on this point see also Greenstein 1982). Though it is true that institutionalization is not necessarily a linear progression from less to more fully institutionalized, the Eisenhower-Kennedy transition is not so much a case of deinstitutionalization as it is one of the cabinet reflecting presidential personality and/or preferences. Therefore, a stronger test of the cabinet's ability to adapt would be to look at its response to other, less personal and more structural changes in the political environment.

The growth of government and the more recent atmosphere of budgetary constraint are two such reinforcing trends that have implications for the cabinet. Major government growth spanned the years from the 1930s until the 1970s. Pressure was put on the cabinet during this period as interests clamored and competed for representation in it. The cabinet effectively responded to this kind of pressure through the creation of new cabinet posts or the upgrading of lower-level agencies to the cabinet level, though one should note that this was accomplished by pressuring Congress, which then legislated change in the cabinet. However, the important point here is that interests viewed representation at the cabinet level as desirable. Like many institutions in the U.S. polity, the cabinet has the capacity to represent interests and expand in order to increase that representation.

On a second level, the cabinet has not dealt well with this government expansion. While it may have been able to represent interests, the cabinet has not been able to integrate or coordinate these effectively. A major issue of the 1930s, and continuing today (Price 1983), is the need to manage the bureaucracy effectively, but the cabinet has not really become a major instrument for such management, in part because of its ability to represent. This, of course, leads to the charge of departmentalism.

A second factor beyond departmentalism, the separation of policy development from implementation, has limited the cabinet role in the coordination of policy and management of the bureaucracy (Price 1983, 99–128). In effect, the creation of the Executive Office of the President in 1939 separated these two functions, giving the first to the Executive Office and the second to the cabinet. This has helped to increase the barrier between the president and the cabinet and, by so doing, has pushed the secretary in the direction of departmental advocate rather than pulling the secretary in the direction of presidential advisor. Another consequence of this separation was that policy development was left without the input of the implementers and their experience as to what were workable or unworkable policies and programs (Hess 1976). Further, removing secretaries from policy development limits their stake in seeing a policy toward success. They are not helping to implement their policies; they are implementing someone else's. This decision to divorce policy development from implementation has surely had major consequences for the cabinet.

A second trend with implications for the cabinet is the impact of budgetary constraint, which probably began in earnest in the 1970s. Budgetary limitations have forced the government to increase its concern with and attention to the cost of government, the effectiveness of programs, the rationalization of competing and often conflicting programs—in short, the problem of policy coordination.

In recent years the cabinet has been seen by some presidents as an important arena where such coordination can be effected. One of the few places in the national government where competing interests meet is at the cabinet level (another being the floor of the Congress). The halls of the bureaucracy are much more limited in terms of the variety of participating interests. Further, at the cabinet level, special interests must also compete with the national interest. Thus, one can account in part for Nixon's and Reagan's focus on the cabinet and the functional grouping of cabinet departments that they proposed and tried. While it is still too early to see just how successful the cabinet can be in helping with policy coordination, one can see presidents trying to revamp their cabinets to help in that chore. This is in part what is meant by institutional adaptability, and the discussion indicates a potential for cabinet adaptability.

Conclusion

The cabinet is hampered critically in its attempts at institutionalizing. First of all, it is not well bounded. Though it is true that most political institutions in the United States have permeable boundaries (note the reforms of the Congress in the 1970s that opened it up to public scrutiny), the cabinet is particularly permeable through its subservient position to the president and Congress. This lack of a well-articulated boundary limits the ability of the cabinet to govern itself.

Similarly, the cabinet is not very coherent as an organization. It is pushed and shoved and shaped by the many different interests of the various departments. Rarely does it take a collective position against the interests. This is due to the lack of collective authority given to the cabinet. It is the president, not the cabinet, who has been elected to office, and thus, it is the president, not the cabinet, who is finally responsible for what happens. Thus, cabinet institutionalization is limited because of the limitations on authority and responsibility.

Yet perhaps the greatest potential for cabinet institutionalization lies in its ability to help in policy coordination and control. This means (1) resisting the interests and departmentalism, and (2) integrating the cabinet into the White House advisory staff. As Hess states, "It is the narrow separation of advice from implementation that is the the most essential reason for an invigorated Cabinet system. . . . A President is bound to receive less enthusiastic support from Cabinet implementers if they are left out of the decisionmaking and are expected to enforce policies that have been formulated behind their backs" (1976, 207). Though the cabinet has not yet progressed far in that direction, the Nixon reform proposals and the Reagan functional cabinet council mechanism show that there are forces attempting to move the cabinet in such a direction, and these forces may be too strong to resist. However, institutionalizing through integration does not make the cabinet a strong institution as much as it attaches it to preexisting institutions. This integrating tendency also undermines cabinet institutionalization by limiting its potential for autonomy.

The potential for the cabinet to adapt and to reorganize into a more coherent body, when contrasted against its permeable boundaries and lack of organizational complexity, reveals one key point about institutionalization—it may proceed at different rates along the different dimensions, and it may be possible for one or another characteristic to develop strongly while the others remain in less developed stages (Kesselman 1970). This may be happening with the cabinet. Forces are motivating it into a more coherent system, but it will never really shake loose from its lack of autonomy or boundedness.

Rather than thinking or hoping for a cabinet on the British model, where it has an important collective role to play, the U.S. cabinet may become more important and more useful to the president if the dual functions of policy development and implementation are better coordinated. The creation of the Executive Office of the President and the other presidential staff agencies held out the promise of greater control of the bureaucracy and government policy. The division of these two aspects of the policy process reinforces the tendency to devolve power in the United States. Integrating the cabinet into the White House may help to resist some of the problems associated with devolution, such as interest group control, departmentalism, and conflicting policies (Hess 1976; Price 1983).

One irony here is that processes in the White House to control these forces have been deinstitutionalizing and politicizing White House staff organizations (Moe 1985; Wyszomirski 1982). That the cabinet may be institutionally enhanced by integrating with deinstitutionalizing bodies not only is ironic but also reveals the basic noninstitutional character of the cabinet.

The cabinet may be thought of as the epitome of a noninstitutional governmental body. What then is the utility of the cabinet, institutionalization theory, and the application of institutionalization theory to the cabinet? First, applying the theory to the cabinet reveals the weaknesses of the cabinet as an institution. This is an important corrective to Fenno's (1959) earlier study, which has led many to think of the cabinet as an institution conforming to Fenno's description of it during the Eisenhower years.

Second, applying the theory to the cabinet reveals the limits of institutionalization theory. This theory derives from work on the sociology of organizations. Polsby's (1968) description of institutions presented above does not include the words *political* or *democratic*. Institutionalization theory is a general theory made to apply to all types of institutions, whether they are political or private, profit making or nonprofit.

However, democratic institutions have particular problems that are addressed unsatisfactorily by institutionalization theory. Not only must democratic political institutions develop the institutional capacity to act, but they must also represent. Representation pressures may undermine institutional maturity as boundaries with the environment are lowered. The reforms of Congress of the 1970s not only deinstitutionalized Congress but also made it more representative and responsive (Rieselbach 1977). Similarly, the politicizing trends in the White House Office and the Executive Office of the President have not only deinstitutionalized those bodies but have also increased their representative character and their political responsibility (Moe 1985).

That the cabinet is not very institutionalized does not make it a useless body. It is more a representative body than an institutionalized one. In a sense this is ironic. It is more natural to think of bureaucracies as more institutionalized than representative, and to think of legislatures as the prime representative political body. The cabinet, however, is the politicized part of the bureaucracy. In fact, the cabinet, and the political appointees of the subcabinet, bring representative pressures to bear on the bureaucracy. The conflict between career executive and political appointee is not only one of time perspective but also one of referent. Career executives aim at service delivery as defined by the institution for which they work. Political appointees aim at service delivery based upon some type of political definition.

The limitation of institutionalization theory is its inability to cope with the deinstitutional pressures of representative democracy and still account for democratic stability. Part of the solution to this problem is found in the genius of the separation of powers. Whereas some bodies are representative, others are institutionally capable. Thus, in the United States it is possible to mix representative government with a government that is institutionally capable and geared for action.

The rest of this book looks at the representative nature of the cabinet. This is the prime importance of the cabinet, not its institutional weaknesses. And viewing it through a representative lens brings into focus the importance of the cabinet. The cabinet is often thought of as unimportant because it is viewed as none too institutional. However, when viewed representationally, it takes on more importance, and from this one will see why presidents continue to return to the theme of cabinet government. What they are really talking about it representative government with a national perspective, a presidential perspective.

★ 3 ★

The Social Bases

of the Cabinet

Chapter 2 focused on the institutional nature of the cabinet and found it lacking in that regard. In the remainder of this book, I change gears and look at the cabinet as a representative body.

It is somewhat difficult to talk of the cabinet, or any other bureaucratic agency, as a representative body composed of representatives because most of the conceptual work on representation relates to legislatures in particular, and cabinet officials do not possess the unambiguous representative position that elected officials do.[1] Specifically, it is easy to identify an elected official's "legal" constituency, that is, the district, the state, or the nation. Except for multimember districts (and states, as in the Senate case), no one else can compete with the elected official as authorized representative. Secretaries, on the other hand, are not officially designated as representatives of this area or that, or this group or that, even though they come from a section of the country or may be a member of an interest group with which the secretary's department must deal. Others may compete with the secretary as spokesperson for an interest. For instance, who is the head of labor, the head of the AFL-CIO or the secretary of labor? Though the head of the AFL-CIO may claim that post, not all unions are members of the federation, and the secretary of labor does occupy a position of importance to the policy goals of labor. Therefore, the secretary of labor may claim labor as his constituency, even though others may do so as well. In contrast, the congressman from the Third District of Ohio has no competitor as congressional representative of that district.

However, this distinction is not as clear or as useful as first appears. While congressmen represent their districts in a formal sense, they may define their constituency in different terms, some of which may transcend district boundaries. For instance, following Fenno's discussion in *Home Style* (1979), congressmen may at one time or another see their constituency as the whole district, the people who compose their electoral support coalition, members of their party, or those individuals who helped recruit them for office and helped them secure and retain that office. Likewise, some congressmen and senators may see their constituency in broader terms, such as environmentalists, the poor, business interests, and the like. Such broad constituencies may be important to congressmen and senators if they are ambitious for the presidency and thus are trying to build national support groups, and/or if they feel that their primary responsibility is to some policy that they desire to see enacted into law. Thus, the term *constituency* may be ambiguous when referring to elected officials as it is somehow ambiguous when referring to a cabinet member.

In her landmark book, *The Concept of Representation* (1967), Pitkin squarely placed responsiveness at the core of any discussion or definition of representation. To Pitkin, the relationship between the represented and the representative is the key, and in this relational sense one can speak of the representativeness or responsiveness of the cabinet and the secretaries.

In further conceptual work, Eulau and Karps (1978) clarify the meaning of responsiveness. First, responsiveness does not imply only that the representative react to the demands of the represented. The representative may initiate the relationship with the represented and lead or direct the thinking of the represented. This representative-to-represented link may be important in building support, which Wahlke (1978) identifies as perhaps more important than the represented making demands on the representative. As I will try to demonstrate, the cabinet officer's importance may derive in part from the ability to generate and maintain support for what he does, and perhaps more crucially, for the administration. When a secretary is unable to do this for the president, often his usefulness declines, and a replacement is sought.

Further, Eulau and Karps (1978) disaggregate the target of responsiveness into one of four kinds, which they call policy responsiveness, service responsiveness, allocative responsiveness, and symbolic responsiveness. Jewell (1982) adds a fifth, communication with the constituency, which overlaps somewhat with symbolic responsiveness.

Policy responsiveness relates to the interaction between the representative and the represented on matters of public policy. This has often been the core concept of representation theory (Eulau and Karps 1978, 63). Service responsiveness deals with particular services that the representative provides to citizens and/or groups, such as casework, which benefit those who are being served. Allocational responsiveness refers to the provision of benefits to the representative's district or clientele groups in anticipation of demands or requests from the represented. Pork barrel legislation is the classic example of an allocatively responsive good. Symbolic responsiveness is a psychological relationship between the represented and the representative. Building trust, support, a feeling that one's voice is being heard are important components of symbolic responsiveness.

For the most part, only policy and symbolic responsiveness are relevant to the cabinet case. Whereas the bureaucracy may serve client groups and citizens and may allocate benefits, for example, by granting contracts, the secretary rarely is engaged in these types of activity.

The cabinet and its secretaries may play important policy roles, however. Though the cabinet as a body cannot make binding collective decisions, the secretaries may, either individually or jointly, provide the president with policy options, guidance, and information. Further, the secretaries may carry out the president's policies in their departments. In this sense, the secretary is indirectly responsive to the public and through the secretary some modicum of public and political control over the career bureaucracy may be possible.

Perhaps more important to the president, though, is the symbolic usefulness of the cabinet as a collective body. Some interest groups claim control over some departments, and the elevation of a person to a department's secretariat who is a member of the interest or has strong ties to it may be symbolically important in building and maintaining the support of that interest for the president and his administration. Presidents may thus build their cabinets with an eye on the electorate and either try to reward voters for past electoral support or attract new voters into the electoral support coalition through their cabinet appointments. In this sense, then, the cabinet's representational usefulness rests more with what it can do for the president than with what it has to offer as a collective body to the public directly. "The president's cabinet" is a good way of looking at the symbolic qualities of the cabinet.

One last point about representation and responsiveness. They can be viewed as either individual or institutional qualities. Pitkin (1967) argues for the supremacy of institutional qualities in determining the quality of representation. We will see that the cabinet possesses important institutional representative qualities. However, secretaries are also important individual representatives. This is especially apparent in discussions of interest group capture of certain cabinet departments. And we shall see that these dual properties, the institutional and the individual, are often in conflict, as the individual often becomes a centrifugal force in cabinet politics. Chapters 3, 4, 5, and 6 deal with these representational concerns.

We begin the investigation of the representational nature of the cabinet by looking at the social backgrounds of the secretaries. The primary utility of data on social background is their ability to inform us about the symbolic representativeness of the cabinet. To a lesser degree, data on social background may reveal something about its policy responsiveness as well.

Most previous research on representation looks at the relationship between the representatives and the represented often conceptualized as congruence (Miller and Stokes 1963) or concurrence (Verba and Nie 1972). Such measures have been criticized because they are unable to determine the causal direction of the relationship (Eulau and Karps 1978). Sometimes the temporal ordering of change in the behaviors and opinions of the representative and the represented enables one to determine causality. In the present study, change over time in the cabinet becomes important information in attempting to assess the cabinet's responsiveness. However, we lack similar data on the represented. This situation stems in part from the tenuous linkage between secretaries and their constituents. Thus, we cannot make definitive statements about responsiveness and representativeness. Further, the source and nature of the agents motivating change in the cabinet will also be open to speculation, yet some sensible educated guesses can be offered.

The use of data on social background represents something of a departure from most studies of political leadership groups, which usually focus on the question of how elitist the group is. Study after study has found that political leaders generally come from society's higher-status strata, that they are generally more educated than the public atlarge, that they tend to be employed in occupations that are accorded more status and income, that they tend to come from families with more in the way of social resources, and the like (Matthews 1954; Putnam 1976). Further, the gross homogeneity of origin of political leaders does not seem to explain differences in the policy preferences among them (Putnam 1976). Consistent findings of the homogeneity of origin and the limited ability of social backgrounds to discriminate the policy attitudes and decisions of political decision makers has almost foreclosed investigation of the role of social backgrounds in determining the character of governmental leaders.

While it is of some interest to note the impressive social standing of secretaries, their social backgrounds can inform one about the representational nature of the cabinet. The way a president builds his cabinet may be indicative of the kinds of voter that the president is trying to link symbolically to his administration (Pious 1979, 240–41). As such, it is not important who the appointed individual is, but rather what group the individual attracts. In this sense presidents appoint cabinet members either to repay certain groups for support in the election or to attract new groups into the president's electoral and policy support coalition. Nixon's "southern strategy"can be viewed in this light—the appointment of southerners, traditionally Democrats, to key positions in the administration, would, it was hoped, attract southern voters to the Republicans. In this sense the electorally symbolic cabinet may be highly responsive in the short term.

The cabinet may also display long-term responsiveness. Rather than showing a response to short-term electoral needs, changes in the social background composition of the cabinet may indicate a response to long-term societal pressures and secular trends. Lasswell (1948) has written, for instance, that there are major historical periods and/or forces that impel change in and transformation of leadership. Lasswell calls these periods skill revolutions, as new environmental and/or political pressures require the leaders in power to adapt. The consequence may mean the evolution or transformation of the leadership's skill base. An understanding of these long-term transformations may impart knowledge not only about the changing symbolic nature of the cabinet, but also about its changing policy preferences and styles.

Three major epochs, each requiring different skills, are evident across U.S. history. The first is the founding and creation of the nation. This epoch required a political leadership well skilled in political matters. One may, therefore, expect to find the cabinet composed largely of professional politicians and others committed to governmental service and political careers.

The Civil War–Reconstruction period ended the epoch of nation building and began the second major epoch, the reform or progressive epoch, in which a major change in orientation toward the government began. Government, it was viewed, could be run scientifically and in an efficient, businesslike manner. Therefore, in this period one should find people recruited from business, in place of the committed politician of the earlier epoch. Here Cincinnatus replaces Caesar. The impact of increased business recruitment of cabinet officials in the second epoch should also lead to a decrease in the length of tenure, as cabinet appointment begins to be viewed as an interruption in a private career. Once the public has been served, these people should, like Cincinnatus, return to private life.

The third, and last epoch is that of big government. Beginning with the New Deal of Franklin Roosevelt, government increased in both size and scope. Managerial and technical skills become more important, and the creation of a large, permanent bureaucracy should be a major source of recruitment for the cabinet. Modern governmental skills can be learned in the government, and there should be less need and desire to recruit from the ranks of the private sector. The government in the third epoch can supply its own skilled officials. During this period one should also see a rise in the length of government and cabinet tenure due to this changed recruitment pattern. Lastly, one should witness a decline in the less specialized skills, such as law, as the requirements of government become more technical and specialized.

Thus, two major types of change will be charted in this chapter, the short-term and the long-term. Short-term changes will primarily refect on the symbolic responsiveness of the cabinet, especially as it relates to presidential electoral needs. Long-term change will reflect on the changing skills required of cabinet members and will give us some indication of changing policy preferences and styles in the cabinet irrespective of presidential electoral politics. Social background data on the age, education, region, and occupation of the secretaries will be used to illustrate these themes.

Data

In this book I present a number of innovations in the study of the cabinet. First, as I have already noted, I look at the cabinet as a representative body. Second, and perhaps as important, I use quantitative career and background data to test these representational ideas. Though quantitative studies of the executive branch are not alien, they are somewhat less common and less developed than those of mass and legislative behavior. I hope to narrow those subdisciplinary differences somewhat with this study and demonstrate that the quantitative research style has something of merit to offer in terms of understanding and theoretical development.

Biographical data on all 468 individuals who have served in the cabinet from George Washington's first administration through December 1984 comprise the data base. The major source for the data is Robert Sobel's *Biographical Directory of the United States Executive Branch*. For data on those people who served after the publication of Sobel's edition (1977), I relied upon the *Who's Who* series, the *Congressional Quarterly*, and government reports.

The Sobel compilation consists of short biographies of the *Who's Who* variety. That is, he presents dates for important career activities of the secretaries. This includes birth and death, educational attendance and attainment, jobs held, and the like. Few interpretive data are offered, though important contributions, such as books written, are also mentioned. Also included are important biographical works on the secretaries. Unsurprisingly, few have been the subject of detailed biographies.

The Sobel data were checked against other lists of cabinet members, and when discrepancies occurred, of which there were a few, other biographical source material on the individual in question was used to reconcile the discrepancy. Also, for some variables of interest, such as political party membership, Sobel's entries are silent. Alternative sources were then used to fill in important data. Among the important sources used in these ways were the *Dictionary of American Biography, The National Cyclopedia of American Biography,* and, for the more recent secretaries, the *Who's Who* series, the *New York Times,* and the *Congressional Quarterly.*

Some data were unrecoverable no matter the source consulted. For instance, it proved impossible to recover data on the religious preferences of most of the secretaries. This data would have been useful when looking at the symbolic representativeness of the cabinet. Yet for a large number of variables documented in this presentation, reliable data on the overwhelming majority of the secretaries was recoverable.

Lastly, before I begin presentation of the data analysis, I should mention the use of significance tests. Strictly speaking, tests of statistical significance are appropriate for samples and not populations. The data on cabinet officials used here represent a population, and on simple tables involving percentages I do not report the tests of statistical significance. However, in the analysis I relied on that information. Hence, when I mention that a difference is significant or large, that judgment is based in part on the significance test, as well as on the size of the difference. Though not reported, the tests of statistical significance proved useful in the analysis. The following sections deal with the age, education, region, and occupation of the secretaries.

Age

It is no surprise to find that cabinet secretaries are generally middle-aged upon appointment. The mean age is 51.8 years, but this mean masks considerable variation. There are the few cases of very young secretaries, such as Alexander Hamilton, who became treasury secretary in his early thirties. Also, there are a few cases of appointments of men in their early seventies. Yet this is the exception. For the secretaries for whom there are reliable birth dates (414 of the 468),[2] 1 was in his twenties upon appointment; 27 (6.5 percent) were in their thirties; 140 (33.8 percent) were in their forties; 161 (38.9 percent) were in their fifties; 82 (19.8 percent) were in their sixties; and 3 were in their seventies.

Age at appointment has several implications. First, as some have argued about presidents, young appointees are likely to be more vigorous and active than older ones. Another implication is that younger appointees may be more ambitious. Classically, studies on ambition use age as an indicator of ambition and argue that young appointees to high-status jobs are more ambitious than older ones (Schlesinger 1966). The older incumbents have had other careers and have less of a future to look forward to. Further, as Laski (1940) pointed out over forty years ago, cabinet posts were not considered careers but instead were viewed as interruptions in careers. For the younger appointee, however, a cabinet post may be viewed as a step in building a political career, a stepping-stone to higher office—the Senate or perhaps the presidency. Such would not be the case for the older occupant, whose career is mostly behind him.

These themes may lead one to suggest that younger appointees will serve longer than older ones. Younger appointees may pursue the job more vigorously and therefore be of more help to a president bent on managing the bureaucracy. Further, they may be using their record as a cabinet member to build a career. Older appointees may be less concerned with their cabinet career and thus likely to leave after shorter terms of service. Correlational analysis indicates a modest negative relationship between age and length of service (Pearson's r = − .096;

significance = .02). Younger appointees do serve for slightly longer than older ones.

Age and Party Eras

Though there is a tendency to appoint middle-aged men to the cabinet, it is not likely that the age patterns wil be the same across the whole history of the nation. For instance, studies of the Congress have found that the average age of members increased in the late 1800s, or about the time of increasing competition for seats, the creation of the senior-ity system, and the lengthening of congressional careers (Witmer 1964; Polsby 1968). The cabinet has not become institutionalized in the same fashion as the Congress, yet historical patterns suggest an aging of the cabinet as well.

One may consider the members of the early cabinets (and the early Congresses also) as members of a new revolutionary leadership, which is typically younger than the established leadership. The cabinet career data indicate that pattern.

To look at this possibility and in order to bring some consistency of presentation across the study, I have divided the history of the nation into five eras that correspond to what are roughly called the five U.S. party eras (Burnham 1970; Beck 1979; Clubb, Flanigan, and Zingale 1980):

(1) 1789–1824
(2) 1825–1860
(3) 1861–1896
(4) 1897–1932
(5) 1933–1984

There is some controversy over these exact demarcations, which Clubb, Flanigan, and Zingale discuss in depth. Also, there is greater contro-versy about whether 1933–84 is one period or two. I consider it one period because such an assumption does no violence to these data (however it may affect other data). I used various cut points dividing era 5 into two eras, but most of the analyses showed no significant differences between suberas. When such differences occur, or a two-period breakdown is warranted, I present the data.

The five-party-era breakdown is useful because it helps to tie these data to other large changes in the political system that do affect the nature of the cabinet, as will be shown throughout. Lastly, the five-party-era breakdown fits comfortably with the three skill epochs mentioned earlier in this chapter. Eras 1 and 2 (1789–1824, 1825–1860) correspond to the first skill epoch, the founding and nation building. Party era 3 (1861–1896) is a transition between the founding and the progressive epochs. Era 4 (1897–1932) corresponds to the progressive epoch, and era 5 (1933–1984) is the period of big government.

The mean age of the cabinet secretaries for the five party eras is as follows:

(1) 1789–1824	43.6
(2) 1825–1860	50.6
(3) 1861–1896	52.9
(4) 1897–1932	54.0
(5) 1933–1984	52.5

The mean age of secretaries in party era 1 was 43.6 years, or 7 years younger than the secretaries of the second or any succeeding era. The last four eras show remarkable similarity in mean ages, ranging from 50.6 to 54.0, a difference of just 3.4 years. Thus, there is a definite aging of the cabinet, and the most likely interpretation is one based on the relative youth of revolutionary leaders when compared to established leaders.[3] This is one indication of the establishment of the constitutional regime relatively early in the nation's history.

Viewed from a more comparative perspective, however, these data also indicate the high levels of circulation and replacement among leaders. Traditionally, studies of the Russian and Chinese revolutions, among others, find that the initially young revolutionary leadership grays but stays in power for very long periods of time: it is not uncommon to find them in power well into their seventies or later (Matthews 1954; Lasswell and Lerner 1965). This does not seem to be the case in the United States. Though the young revolutionary leadership did age, its age topped off at about fifty, which is well below the Russian and Chinese experiences.

The comparative youth and revolutionary nature of the cabinet officers of party era 1 also lead to the suspicion that terms of service were longer in the early cabinets. This suspicion is borne out by the data displayed in table 1. Whereas service spanned 69 months on average in era 1, it dropped to 27 months in era 2 and hovered in the 34–40 month range over eras 3, 4, and 5. Part of this drop may be accounted for by the average length of presidential service. Here presidential service is viewed in terms of administrations because of the tendency of presidents who succeeded those who died in office to keep the cabinet officers of the deceased president for at least a modest period. Therefore, the Harrison–Tyler, Taylor–Fillmore, Lincoln–A. Johnson, Garfield–Arthur, McKinley–T. Roosevelt (first term only), Harding–Coolidge, F. Roosevelt (last term only)–Truman, Kennedy– Johnson, and Nixon–Ford administrations are each counted as single units.

Whereas it is true that average length of presidential service dropped from era 1 to era 2 and stayed low in era 3, era 4 and especially era 5 saw increases in length of presidential tenure. One cannot account for the dramatic drop in cabinet service by length of presidential service.

To return to the early finding of the inverse relationship between age of cabinet members and length of service, it may be that that relationship is masking the impact of the party eras on length of service. A multiple regression was run of the form Y (length of service in months) = constant + B_1 (age) + B_2(party era). Here a dummy variable was created for party era such that 0 equals era 1 and 1 equals eras 2, 3, 4, and 5. I ran other equations with dummy variables for each of the party eras, but the equations showed that the only real difference among them was that between the first and all the others. The results of the equation are:

$$Y = 69.2 - .39 \, (\text{Age}) \quad -33.25 \quad (\text{Party era dummy})$$
$$(.22) \qquad\qquad (6.22)$$
$$\text{Multiple } r = .27 \quad R^2 = .07 \quad F = 15.9$$
$$\text{Adjusted } R^2 = .07$$

TABLE 1
Length of Cabinet Tenure by Party Era
(in months)

	Era 1	Era 2	Era 3	Era 4	Era 5	All Years
All	69	27	34	38	40	38
(N)	(38)	(72)	(96)	(86)	(124)	(416)
Initial Appointee	63	29	37	50	54	45
(N)	(11)	(37)	(49)	(40)	(51)	(188)
Replacements	71	25	31	28	30	34
(N)	(27)	(35)	(47)	(46)	(73)	(228)

Note: The five party eras are as follows:
  (1) 1789–1824: the founding era;
  (2) 1825–1860: the nation-building era;
  (3) 1861–1896: the transitional era;
  (4) 1897–1932: the progressive era;
  (5) 1933–1984: the era of big government.

The numbers in parentheses are the standard errors. The results indicate that the age-service relationship is a function of the party era-service relationship. Age is not statistically significant when party era is used as a control variable. The t value for the age variable is 1.77, which is less than the 2.00 that is often used as a conventional test of the significance of the t coefficient.

Again, these results show the revolutionary leadership nature of the early cabinets. Like other revolutionary leaderships, this one persists in office longer than succeeding ones, but it must still be distinguished from those of Russia and China in that its tenure is considerably shorter, an indication of the responsiveness to democratic pressures and the circulation and replacement of leaders that competitive democracy compels.

In these data we may see some hints of symbolic and policy responsiveness on the part of the cabinet. Symbolic responsivieness may come from the replacement of the early leadership as well as from its initial longevity. Its longevity may provide the budding nation with people who are identified with it. This in turn may help the public build an identification with the new nation. In other words, the people initially identify with the new nation's leaders, and this identification is transferred from these heroes to the idea of a nation.

Policy responsiveness may also be hinted at. Replacement of the revolutionary leadership through processes other than natural attrition, such as elections and rotation of parties and presidents in office, indicates a responsiveness to the institutions of democracy. Though this transformation does not indicate the policy directions that it may have motivated, it does signal the lack of insulation of this appointive leadership from democratic pressures. Throughout, other signs of democratic responsiveness will also be demonstrated.

Age and Political Party

To round out the discussion of age, let us turn to the relationship between age and party. Table 2 displays the age distributions of cabinet members by their own party and by their president's party. I should note here that it was not always possible to ascertain the secretary's party. To determine this, because registration and preference data were not available, I had to rely upon more informal membership and activity data. Therefore, I am unable to distinguish between true independents and those who sided with the one party but did not show that preference in an active manner. Thus, independents and closet partisans are lumped together in a category labeled "Don't Know or Not Sure." However, use of multiple sources, as I mentioned earlier in this chapter, allowed me to determine the party affiliation of 89.8 percent of the secretaries. The remaining 10.2 percent represent true independents and those for whom the information is missing. It is interesting that the percentage of missing data was highest in the party era 1, when party loyalties were just beginning to form and were most fluid. This finding helps to ensure confidence in the party variable.

Cabinet officers from the early Federalist party are somewhat younger than those from the Democratic-Republican and the later parties. This may indicate that the transformation from a youthful revolutionary leadership into a democratically responsive one occurred even earlier than the previous data suggested. Similarly, the Federalist presidents

TABLE 2

Age by Political Party

	Party Era	Dem.	Repub.	Dem.-Repub.	Whig	Federalist
Secretary's party	1	—	—	53.5	—	46.5
	2	54.1	—	—	51.1	—
	3	54.5	56.9	—	—	—
	4	52.4	57.9	—	—	—
	5	56.1	57.7	—	—	—
Grand mean		54.7	57.4	53.5	51.1	46.5
President's party	1	—	—	48.4	—	39.8
	2	55.1	—	—	50.9	—
	3	53.0	56.8	—	—	—
	4	51.5	57.3	—	—	—
	5	56.6	56.3	—	—	—
Grand mean		55.0	53.7	48.4	50.9	39.8

Note: For party eras, see table 1.

Washington and Adams appointed secretaries who were almost 9 years younger than those appointed by the Jeffersonian Democratic-Republican presidents. The considerable youth of the cabinets of the Federalist presidents is in part a function of youth of Alexander Hamilton.

The age-party relationship may be confounded by time. To control for this possibility, table 2 also presents breakdowns for each of the party eras. Again, other than the already noted youth of the Federalists and the subsequent aging of the cabinet over time, no party-related age differences emerge. This is true for breakdowns by both secretary's and appointing president's party. Lastly, and somewhat trivially, Republicans tend to be slightly older than Democrats, to judge from either secretarial or presidential breakdowns. And while party era 4 shows the largest partisan difference in age, it is still trivial in magnitude. More importantly, both parties have been consistently and historically middle-aged.

Education

The educational attainment of the cabinet officers starkly reveals their position as a socially privileged group. It is almost a requisite to have some college education. Fully 80.8 percent of the secretaries had at least some college education, and 34 percent earned advanced degrees. Clearly this is a level of education well beyond that of the public at large. In 1970, for instance, only 11 percent of the American public, according to the Census Bureau, were college graduates, and another 10 percent had some college exposure. Further, the more prestigious and well-known colleges are well represented. Looking at the prestige of the colleges is important because it provides a clue to the social class from which the secretary came (Prewitt and McAllister 1976).

Table 3 lists the most frequently attended colleges for both the undergraduate and graduate training of the secretaries. Looking just at the Big Three—Harvard, Yale, and Princeton—19.4 percent of all secretaries and 24.8 percent of those with only undergraduate degrees attended these three schools. Graduate education shows similar tendencies—27.5 percent of those who earned advanced degrees went to Harvard or Yale.

One can look at these educational data a little more systematically by arranging the colleges into three groups: the established prestige schools, the less established prestige schools, and the nonprestige schools. The procedure followed here is similar to the one followed by Prewitt and McAllister (1976) in their study of the executive leadership from 1920 to 1970. The established prestige colleges are those older schools long known and highly thought of in the nation. These include the Ivy League, other small eastern colleges such as Amherst and Williams, and other scattered colleges throughout the nation with long histories of excellence, such as Oberlin and Stanford. The less established prestige schools mostly include the large urban universities, such as George Washington and Boston universities, and the major state university campuses. The nonprestigious campuses include the state agricultural colleges and small, relatively unknown colleges. While some may disagree with placement of individual schools, the categorization does provide us with a rough indication of the prestige of the colleges attended by the cabinet officers.

TABLE 3
Most Frequently Attended Colleges
(in percentages)

	N	All	BA		N	All	Post-BA
Harvard	37	7.9	10.1	Harvard	36	7.7	22.5
Yale	29	6.2	7.9	Columbia	9	1.9	5.6
Princeton	25	5.3	6.8	Yale	8	1.7	5.0
Michigan	9	1.9	2.5	Texas	6	1.3	3.8
North Carolina	9	1.9	2.5	George Washington	5	1.1	3.1
Columbia	8	1.7	2.2	California, Berkeley	5	1.1	3.1
Pennsylvania	8	1.7	2.2	Michigan	4	.9	2.5
William and Mary	8	1.7	2.2	Cincinnati	4	.9	2.5
Dartmouth	6	1.3	1.6	Virginia	4	.9	2.5
Dickinson College	6	1.3	1.6				
Union	5	1.1	1.4				
Stanford	5	1.1	1.4				
Amherst	4	.9	1.1				
Brown	4	.9	1.1				
West Point	4	.9	1.1				
Chicago	4	.9	1.1				
Virginia	4	.9	1.1				
Cumberland	4	.9	1.1				
California, Berkeley	4	.9	1.1				
(N)		(468)	(367)			(468)	(158)

Using this rough indicator, 58.0 percent of the secretaries who attended college went to the established prestige schools, 21.2 percent to the less prestigious schools, and 20.9 percent to the nonprestigious institutions. For all secretaries, 45.1 percent attended established prestige schools, 16.5 percent less established prestige schools, and 16.4 percent nonprestige schools. The same pattern is evident for graduate education. Of those who received advanced degrees, 53.2 percent went to established prestige schools, 29.7 percent went to less established prestige schools, and 17.1 percent attended nonprestige schools. Looking at all secretaries, one finds that 17.9 percent received advanced degrees from established prestige schools, 10.0 percent from less established prestige institutions, and 5.8 percent from the nonprestige institutions. Again, one sees a picture of a privileged group that not only attended college at higher rates than the public at large but also went to the most prestigious schools in the nation at rates greater than one would find for the college-going population.

Education and Party Era

Just as the educational attainment of the public has increased over the course of U.S history, so also has the cabinet's educational level increased, even though these leaders started with high levels of education. Relevant data are displayed in table 4. Even prior to the twentieth century, fully one-half or more of the secretaries graduated from college. By party era 5 college experience is almost universal. Almost 93 percent in era 5 went to college, 75 percent graduated from college, and 60 percent held advanced degrees.

Some sketchy data may allow us to compare the educational background of the cabinet secretaries with that of the public. Data on the public's educational attainment goes back only to the late 1800s, and it is not as complete or detailed as that presented for the cabinet, yet some comparison is possible. For each of the last three party eras, I choose the highest percentage of citizens who earned high school diplomas, as reported in the *Historical Statistics of the United States,* for comparison. This is the only long series of historical educational data available. For

TABLE 4

Educational Level by Party Era
(in percentages)

	Era 1	Era 2	Era 3	Era 4	Era 5	All Years
Less than high school	12.5	9.2	8.2	4.5	2.4	6.0
High school graduate	22.5	21.1	17.5	11.4	4.2	12.6
Some college	17.5	6.6	7.2	10.2	7.8	8.8
College graduate	45.0	56.6	47.4	34.1	24.6	38.0
Graduate school	—	6.6	18.6	39.8	60.5	34.0
No information	2.5	—	1.0	—	.6	.6

Note: For party eras, see table 1.

the three eras, the relevant figures are: era 3, 3.5 percent; era 4, 32.1 percent; and era 5, 75.6 percent. Clearly the cabinet easily outstrips the public—the cabinet's college graduation levels far exceed the high school graduation levels for the public. By any measures, this is surely an educational elite.

However, though both the cabinet and the public show increasing levels of education, it is difficult to argue that the increases on the part of the cabinet were motivated by the same forces that changed those of the public. The cabinet began as an educational elite. Those increases that occurred were relatively small and occurred mostly at the top end of the educational system, that is, at the college to graduate school levels. Mass educational improvement, though great in participation, is more modest in level reached.

Education and Party

Though education may be important for cabinet membership, the two current major parties are based in two different social classes, and education and social class are closely related. Therefore, one may expect the differences in social class of the two major modern parties to be reflected in their cabinets as well. This is not to suggest that Democrats will not possess high levels of education; rather, Republicans will display even higher levels. Tables 5 and 6 report on some of these data.

The data in table 5 indicate little difference in the level of education of secretaries chosen by presidents of the two modern parties. The earlier parties show cabinets of somewhat lower, though still high, levels, but this is a function of the slightly lower levels of education of secretaries, elites generally, and the public in the earlier decades of the Republic. Democratic and Republican presidents display virtually identical preferences for the level of education of their secretaries.

Again, time may mask some possible party-related differences. Table 6 presents the percentage of college graduates by party for each party era. For the most part, no strong presidential party recruitment effects are found. Both modern parties show increases in educational level over time, though the Republican trend seems slightly speedier than that for the Democrats. By party era 4, Republicans hold a modest edge,

TABLE 5

Educational Level by President's Party
(in percentages)

	Dem.	Repub.	Dem.-Repub.	Whig	Federalist
Less than high school	5.6	4.7	7.1	14.7	7.1
High school graduate	11.9	12.7	25.0	11.8	28.6
Some college	7.9	7.0	14.3	11.8	21.4
College graduate	32.8	38.8	50.0	50.0	42.9
Graduate school	41.2	38.3	3.6	11.8	—
(N)	(177)	(214)	(28)	(34)	(14)

TABLE 6

College Graduates by President's Party
(in percentages)

Party Era	Dem.	Repub.	Dem.-Repub.	Whig	Federalist
1	—	—	53.6	—	42.9
2	61.0	—	—	61.8	—
3	69.0	67.7	—	—	—
4	68.4	76.1	—	—	—
5	84.9	86.1	—	—	—

Note: For party eras, see table 1.

with almost 8 percent more of their secretaries graduating from college and/or going to graduate school. However, by era 5 the difference vanishes. Also, of the two earliest parties, Democratic-Republicans recruit a slightly higher percentage of college-educated secretaries than Federalists, but again, the difference is not pronounced or significant.

Similarly, there is no significant difference in the educational attainment of secretaries of the two modern parties (table 7). If anything, Democratic secretaries possess a slightly higher percentage of advanced degrees than Republican ones. Again, secretaries of the three earlier parties display slightly lower levels of education, but again, this is a function of time. If the parties are rooted in different classes, this is not obvious from the educational level of their cabinet officers. Mere inspection of education paints a picture of highly educated leadership in both parties.

Again, breakdowns by party were inspected to check for time-related effects. These breakdowns are shown on table 8. Again, the general finding of no strong party-time differences emerges. However, some weak relationships are worth noting. Democratic-Republican secretaries are slightly more educated than Federalists in party era 1 and Whigs display somewhat higher levels of education than Democrats in era 2. The two modern parties track together quite closely, with the only differences occurring in era 3, when Democrats slightly surpass Republicans. But by era 4 this difference disappears.

TABLE 7
Educational Level by Secretary's Party
(in percentages)

	Dem.	Repub.	Dem.-Repub.	Whig	Federalist
Less than high school	6.5	6.4	9.5	6.9	—
High school graduate	11.9	11.2	14.3	13.8	33.3
Some college	6.5	8.0	14.3	6.9	11.1
College graduate	33.9	39.0	57.1	62.1	55.5
Graduate school	41.1	35.3	4.8	10.3	—

TABLE 8
College Graduates by Secretary's Party
(in percentages)

Party Era	Dem.	Repub.	Dem.-Repub	Whig	Federalist
1	—	—	61.9	—	55.5
2	60.0	—	—	72.4	—
3	75.0	62.3	—	—	—
4	73.7	74.1	—	—	—
5	88.0	81.2	—	—	—

Note: For party eras, see table 1.

TABLE 9
College Prestige by Political Party
(in percentages)

		Dem.	Repub.	Dem.-Repub	Whig	Federalist
President's party	Established prestige	35.8	42.3	53.3	44.4	42.4
	Newer prestige	22.9	20.9	3.4	11.1	—
	Nonprestige	17.1	15.0	—	8.3	—
	No college	25.4	22.4	46.4	38.3	57.6
Secretary's party	Established prestige	45.8	54.0	75.0	51.7	66.7
	Newer prestige	16.1	14.4	—	10.3	—
	Nonprestige	17.9	9.7	—	13.9	—
	No college	20.2	21.9	25.0	24.1	33.3

Party differences in education may show up, though, if one looks at the prestige of the college attended. College prestige may be a better indicator of class background, since the more prestigious and expensive the school, the more likely that its student body will be skewed in an upper-class direction (Prewitt and McAllister 1976). Table 9 considers this possibility. There is some very slight support for this contention. First, we must disregard the prestige comparisons of the early parties. Most of the colleges that existed early on have become our current prestige schools, and my prestige classification is not able to take into account historical prestige rankings among colleges. And, considering the few colleges in existence then, it may not make much sense to distinguish among them in this way.

Comparing Democrats and Republicans reveals some party differences. Republicans are slightly more likely to attend prestige schools (54.0 percent to 45.8 percent) and somewhat less likely to attend nonprestige ones (9.7 percent to 17.9 percent), but other than these modest differences, what is most striking is how similar Republicans and Democrats look. Both parties recruit more heavily from the prestige ranks than from anywhere else, and the precentage differences in recruitment from different types of colleges is modest at best.

Time, however, may affect the finding of party similarities. Occa-

TABLE 10

Attendance at Established Prestige Colleges by Political Party
(in percentages)

	Party Era	Dem.	Repub.	Dem.-Repub.	Whig	Federalist
President's	1	—	—	53.3	—	42.4
party	2	41.5	—	—	44.4	—
	3	36.7	36.9	—	—	—
	4	36.8	53.7	—	—	—
	5	44.2	45.0	—	—	—
Secretary's	1	—	—	75.0	—	66.7
party	2	44.4	—	—	51.7	—
	3	44.0	32.8	—	—	—
	4	36.8	58.6	—	—	—
	5	42.7	48.5	—	—	—

Note: For party eras, see table 1.

sionally, for the two modern parties, there are important party differences in type of college. According to table 10, party era 3 shows no presidential party differential in recruitment from the established prestige colleges, but by era 4 differences between the parties grow, as might be expected. Republican presidents are more likely to recruit from the established prestige schools than Democratic presidents by almost 17 percent. This may reflect the growing class tensions between the parties of the early part of the twentieth century: the populist Democrats and the middle- and upper-class Republican progressives. By era 5 these differences recede to insignificance, which may be a function of the diffusion of college experience throughout the populace as well as the greater Republican heterodoxy in appointing secretaries from a wider social spectrum. These findings are duplicated when the focus changes to the secretary.

However, the main information from the data is the very high levels of education of secretaries. Such levels clearly rank them as an educational elite. Further, party differences are slight, though they occasionally emerge when we employ college prestige to locate class backgrounds. These data indicate some limits to responsiveness. Rather than the cabinet looking like the public when it comes to education, a college education seems a requisite for the job. Though the cabinet is symbolically representative in some ways, education is one characteristic generally insulated from these representative pressures.

Region

Traditionally, party electoral strength has varied by region. Regionalism in U.S. politics takes on implications beyond mere election results, however. The depth of regional divisions across history has made region a major force in attracting and/or repelling voters. Thus, region has important symbolic implications, some of which may affect the cabinet, as people notice where a secretary comes from. However, regional divisions connote more than symbolic political appeal; they also connote policy differences at times.

The key regional division in the United States separates North from South. The severity of this division is apparent by just noting the Civil War. For many years after that, northerner and southerner were suspicious of each other, and post-Civil War politics revolved in part around these suspicions and animosities. For nearly a century after the war, the South was dominated by one political party, the Democrats, to the almost total exclusion of the Republican party. And in the North, the Democratic party was at a severe membership disadvantage until the Depression of the 1930s transformed the substance of politics there.

Regional divisions after the Civil War were not limited to symbolic appeals to history but also reflected policy differences. A number of policy areas divided the two areas, including import policy, agricultural support policy, and industrial policy, but perhaps the signal policy difference related to race. Thus, the appointment of a southerner to the cabinet would connote to voters the president's attitudes to the rebellious region, and might also indicate his policy preferences on a number of fronts. In general, southern representation would indicate a conservative direction on racial affairs and state autonomy from the national government.

Other regional divisions exist and will be discussed, though none equals the North-South division in depth, endurance, and impact. Region serves, then, as an important clue concerning the symbolic and policy representativeness of the cabinet.

Table 11 shows the regional distribution of secretaries and breakdowns by party era. I define the four major regions in the following way: *East*—Delaware, Pennsylvania, New Jersey, Connecticut, Massachusetts, Maryland, New Hampshire, Vermont, Maine, New York, Rhode Island; *South*—Florida, Georgia, South Carolina, North Carolina, Virginia, Alabama, Mississippi, Tennessee, Louisiana, Arkansas, Texas; *Midwest*—Kentucky, West Virginia, Ohio, Michigan, Indiana, Illinois, Wisconsin, Minnesota, Iowa, Kansas, Missouri, Oklahoma, Nebraska, North Dakota, South Dakota; *West*—Montana, Wyoming, Colorado, New Mexico, Arizona, Utah, Idaho, Nevada, Washington, Oregon, California, Alaska, Hawaii.

First, traditionally the most populated region, the East, is most heavily represented in the cabinet, and the least populated region (until recently), the West, is least well represented. But, if population is used as a base, the South is most clearly underrepresented. This finding can be clarified by looking at the historical transformation of the regional composition of the cabinet.

In the cabinets prior to the Civil War, the South was well represented, but from then until the New Deal, the South, with about one-

TABLE 11
Region of Origin by Party Era
(in percentages)

	Era 1	Era 2	Era 3	Era 4	Era 5	All Years
East	64.1	47.4	45.7	44.7	44.1	44.7
Midwest	7.7	17.1	42.6	36.5	24.3	26.5
South	28.2	35.3	9.6	8.2	15.1	16.5
West	—	—	2.1	10.6	16.4	8.0

Note: For party eras, see table 1.

TABLE 12
Region of Origin by Secretary's Party
(in percentages)

	Dem.	Repub.	Dem.-Repub.	Whig	Federalist
East	37.5	39.4	57.1	48.3	66.7
Midwest	23.6	41.7	4.8	20.7	—
South	28.4	8.5	38.1	31.0	33.3
West	6.6	11.4	—	—	—

third of the nation's population, was almost frozen out of the cabinet. The secessionist South was stigmatized until the New Deal, when the new Democratic coalition, which included it, came to power and reintroduced southerners into the cabinet. But even in the most modern period, southerners are drastically underrepresented.

Data in table 12 indicate that secretaries of the different parties are recruited most heavily from the region of the party's strength, except that there is a tendency to overrepresent the East. Only Republicans show another region, the Midwest, surpassing the East in recruitment, but this difference is rather slight (2.3 percent). This eastern overrepresentation is probably a consequence of the great population of the East and its electoral significance.

The other regions display the regional biases of the parties, though. Republican secretaries are more likely than Democrats to come from the Midwest. Significant numbers of Democratic secretaries hail from the South, whereas only a few Republicans have southern roots. To look at the data slightly differently, for the secretaries who are either Democrats or Republicans, over 77 percent of the southerners are Democrats. This is a clear indication of the historic weakness of the Republican party in the South and the impact of the Civil War on the regional bases of the two modern parties.

Breakdowns by era show the parties' regional proclivities quite strikingly. Results are reported in table 13 for the last three party eras. The proportion of Republican secretaries from the East has remained rather stable since the Civil War period. However, across the same time,

TABLE 13
Region of Origin by Secretary's Party and Party Era
(in percentages)

	Era 3		Era 4		Era 5	
	Dem.	Repub.	Dem.	Repub.	Dem.	Repub.
East	48.0	42.3	36.8	45.5	45.0	44.1
Midwest	28.0	49.2	36.8	38.1	22.5	30.5
South	24.0	5.1	21.1	1.8	19.7	8.5
West	—	3.4	5.3	14.5	12.7	16.9

Note: For party eras, see table 1.

midwestern representation declined from almost one-half in era 3 to less than one-third in era 5. At first, midwestern declines were matched by western gains,, and without any southern gains. Yet, in era 5, Republican secretaries in significant though not overwhelming numbers come from the South. In these figures one can observe the nationalization of the Republican party.

Democrats, like Republicans, were parochial in the sense of having no western representatives during party era 3. However, western representation has grown, but at the expense of all of the other regions. Democrats seem to show more regional fluidity over time, with less eastern dominance in era 4. But, more importantly, like Republicans, they display a nationalizing tendency. By era 5 the parties have come to resemble each other in regional composition, though the Democrats are slightly more southern and less midwestern than the Republicans.

The cabinets of presidents of different parties echo the findings about the secretaries themselves. Table 14 gives these data. Again, the East is similarly represented in both Democratic and Republican presidential cabinets, but the South is almost absent from those of Republican presidents. And, though Democratic presidents are less reliant on midwesterners than Republicans are, the West also plays a marginally bigger role in Republican than Democratic administrations.

These party-regional biases become even more apparent when the analysis breaks down these presidential cabinets by party era as well as

TABLE 14
Region of Origin by President's Party
(in percentages)

	Dem.	Repub.	Dem.-Repub.	Whig	Federalist
East	45.2	45.8	51.9	52.9	61.5
Midwest	25.0	35.5	14.8	14.7	—
South	22.0	7.4	33.3	32.4	38.5
West	7.7	11.3	—	—	—

by region. Table 15 considers this more complex relationship. Democrats of all eras appoint many easterners, and after the Civil War, Democratic presidents increased their reliance upon midwesterners, mostly at the expense of southerners. In party era 2 almost 36 percent of Democratic cabinet officials were southern. After the Civil War this number was cut in half, and has not grown at all. Era 5 shows an increase of western representation in Democratic cabinets, a reflection of the great population growth of the West during that period.

Republican presidents show similar regional appointment biases by recruiting most heavily from their party's regions of electoral strength. Again, the East is heavily represented, and at about the same rate as for Democratic presidents. The Midwest is more heavily represented in Republican cabinets than Democratic ones, but midwestern representation has been declining, mostly because of the great rates of growth, in both population and cabinet representation of the West. In party eras 3 and 4, the South was almost totally excluded from Republican cabinets, and though some gains have been made in era 5, the percentage of southerners is still quite small. These data reveal starkly the impact of regionalism on U.S. electoral politics and on the cabinet. Regional recruitment appears consistent with the regional strengths of the parties.

Lastly, consider the impact of presidential region on the regional composition of the cabinet. One may suggest that presidents will choose disproportionately from their own region of origin. This would be in part a reflection of regional style differences and the decentralized nature of the party system, which forces presidents to build govern-

TABLE 15

Region of Origin by President's Party and Party Era

(in percentages)

	Democratic				Republican			
	Era 2	Era 3	Era 4	Era 5	Era 2	Era 3	Era 4	Era 5
East	46.2	50.0	40.0	43.6	—	44.4	46.2	45.2
Midwest	17.9	30.0	35.0	24.4	—	47.6	36.9	24.7
South	35.9	16.7	20.0	17.9	—	6.3	4.6	11.0
West	—	3.3	5.0	14.1	—	1.6	12.3	19.2
(N)	(39)	(30)	(20)	(78)	—	(63)	(65)	(73)

Note: For party eras, see table 1.

TABLE 16
Secretary's Region by President's Region
(in percentages)

Secretary's Region	President's Region				
	East	Midwest	South	West	Mean
East	49.5	42.9	50.4	45.8	46.9
Midwest	28.0	37.4	16.5	25.0	27.8
South	18.7	10.4	27.6	8.3	17.3
West	3.7	9.2	5.5	20.8	8.1

ments on their own and with only minimal party input (MacKenzie 1981). Examples of this are Kennedy's "Boston Irish Mafia," Carter's "Georgia Mafia," and Reagan's "California Connection."

Some relevant data are supplied in table 16. These data show that presidents are biased toward secretaries from their own region, with one major exception: presidents from all regions choose similar numbers of secretaries from the east. Southerners are slightly more prone to pick other southerners, midwesterners to pick other midwesterners, and westerners to pick other westerners. Eastern presidents show no such regional tendency and recruit from all regions at about the average rates. Also, while southern presidents choose southerners, they tend not to appoint western or midwestern secretaries very often. And midwesterners and westerners tend not to appoint many southerners to their cabinets.

Region plays an important part in politics in the United States, and this is reflected in the cabinet. Parties and presidents recruit secretaries from their regions of strength. Such a bias may indicate an attempt to represent and link voters from those regions symbolically to the competing parties and changing administrations. But these regional differences may have more than mere symbolic implications, for the different regions sit on different sides on many important issues. Thus, regional distinctions among the parties may indicate policy differences as well, which, through the route of regionalism, may find their way into cabinet politics and policy formation. In this sense, then, the cabinet may again play a representative role in U.S. politics.

Occupation

Occupation, like education, is an indicator of class status, and secretaries tend to hold relatively high-status jobs prior to appointment. Only a few scattered secretaries held menial laborer or other lower-class occupations. But occupation presents us with information about more than the elite nature of the cabinet. It also relates to the question of the skills of the secretary, and it may provide us with clues to the responsive abilities of the cabinet.

Scholars have looked at the skills of a political elite over time to chart its rise and/or fall (Mosca 1939; Lasswell 1948; Prewitt and McAllister 1976). Previous sections have noted some important transformations of the cabinet, its aging after the accession to power of the youthful leaders of the Revolutionary War and Constitution-writing periods, its increasing education, and the virtual exclusion of southerners after the Civil War. Another and perhaps more fundamental transformation has also occurred, which relates to the changing skills of the secretaries.

External social, economic, technological, and political forces often require responses on the part of leaders, and one possible response may be an alteration in the composition of the leadership in power. In democratic theory, elections and public opinion serve as vehicles to promote the transformation of the leadership, and the history of the cabinet reflects these external and democratic forces.

One may hypothesize the following sequence of events that would lead to skill transformations of the cabinet. In the early epoch, the period of nation building, leaders with the necessary political skills to build a nation were required. Some hints of this need were mentioned earlier in the relative length of cabinet service of the early secretaries.

By the conclusion of the Civil War, the traumas of nation building were concluded; the national government now reigned supreme over the states and localities. But at this same time, the nation entered a new epoch, one based on economic expansion and progressive ideals that government should, and could, be run scientifically and efficiently. Professional politicians were no longer needed. Now what was required was people with business and scientific training who could apply their special skills to the problem of government. Such people were to be found in the private sector.

The forces of economic growth and industrialization created pressures that were realized and acted upon by the government, at first slowly and in small steps, with the creation of some of the regulatory commissions, and later with the welfare state as a solution to the economic failures of the private sector during the Great Depression. The size, complexity, and scope of government of the New Deal and post–New Deal era required leaders trained in administration and government, and new government leaders recruited from the bureaucracies of the government itself ascended to power.

An alternative to the above view is that the primary forces for change are not secular and long-term but are mediated by party competition and the electoral fortunes of the parties. Therefore, one is more likely to find temporary changes in the cabinet that reflect the alternation of parties in the White House. If this is the case, one should notice the ascendancy of business and the private sector during Republican administrations. In contrast, during Democratic administrations, with their more favorable attitude toward big, positive government, secretaries should be recruited more heavily from the ranks of government. The following section will test these competing claims, relying on evidence of recruitment and exit patterns, as well as their implications for tenure in office.

The two dynamics of change outlined above also related to our primary question, the responsiveness and representativeness of the cabinet. Both symbolic and policy representation can be seen by looking at occupational background. Such an exercise has been attempted in the previous sections on education, age, and region. However, the analysis in this section can be made more sensitive by testing two competing mechanisms that impel cabinet change: the long-term secular and the electoral. Assessment of the relative impact of secular versus electoral change will reveal a major component of the political nature of the cabinet.

Occupation and Recruitment Patterns

Before analyzing occupational patterns and cabinet service, one must develop an occupational typology with relevance to the topic at hand. A typology of specific occupations may be too detailed and unwieldy for easy analysis and presentation. One based on economic sectors may make more sense. A number of such typologies have been offered (Prewitt and McAllister 1976; Heclo 1978). The one used here is based upon those of Prewitt and McAllister and of Heclo but is adapted to my purposes. The discussion to follow details these points.

Precabinet job experience was categorized into four classifications; government, law, business, and education. Government includes any government post; also included are the many party posts. Law is limited to membership in a law firm and is a separate category because of the oft mentioned importance of lawyers to the operation of the U.S. government. The educational category includes teachers, educational administrators, ministers of religion, and foundation executives. The business category includes all other jobs, for instance, corporate executives, small businessmen, bankers, and the like. Though part of the private sector, educational and foundation experience differ sufficiently from the business world to be classified as a separate category.

These four categories provide one with a crude index of skills that have some relevance to the cabinet specifically, and to the government more generally. Law, though specialized, is general in its applicability across problems and issues. Education, on the other hand, is specialized and generally technical. The business category is primarily related to the particular types of management and business skills developed in the private sector. The government category combines both political and administrative skills, and, when necessary, I will try to disaggregate these.

This classification is similar to that of Prewitt and McAllister (1976) except for my differentiation of private sector and government sector administrative skills. Also, I make a distinction between primary occupation and last job prior to cabinet appointment. Primary occupation is similar to Prewitt and McAllister's concept of career space.

Table 17 presents some initial data on the occupations of the secretaries. Surprisingly at first, and counter to the interest group capture and the amateur theories of the U.S. government, one finds significant numbers of secretaries whose major occupation was government service and/or politics (37.3 percent). Still, the bulk of the cabinet is recruited from the other categories (business, 25.6 percent; law, 27.8 percent;

TABLE 17
Primary Occupation by Party Era
(in percentages)

	Era 1	Era 2	Era 3	Era 4	Era 5	All Years
Law	12.5	23.7	34.0	37.5	24.6	27.8
Government	70.0	71.0	48.4	23.9	25.2	37.3
Business	15.0	5.3	13.4	34.1	40.1	25.6
Education	—	—	3.1	4.5	10.2	7.3

Note: For party eras, see table 1.

education, 7.3 percent), and as expected, the legal professional provides a large group of cabinet personnel. When compared to the European cabinets, which are almost exclusively composed of politicians and heads of parties, the U.S. cabinet indeed appears amateurish, yet the large representation of members with primary government careers should not be overlooked.

If one looks at the last job prior to cabinet appointment, rather than at the primary occupation, one finds that precabinet government experience is widespread (see table 18). Here 67.7 percent of the secretaries have some government experience, whereas business experience drops to 13.9 percent, law to 12.0 percent, and education to 4.7 percent. Clearly, there is a tendency to recruit directly from the ranks of those already in the government. The citizen who becomes a secretary without any previous government experience is the exception rather than the rule, and a fairly rare exception at that (1 of 7). Though not necessarily government professionals, secretaries have some government experience before their cabinet tenure begins.

The discussion of the skills revolution and the transformation of the cabinet identified three epochs. The first, the founding, should emphasize governmental and political expertise. The second, the reform or progressive period, should emphasize business management skills, and the third, the period of big government, should emphasize government administrative skills.

The five party eras are useful as time demarcations to test the skills revolution thesis. The first two party eras may be considered the period

TABLE 18
Last Job Before Appointment
(in percentages)

	Era 1	Era 2	Era 3	Era 4	Era 5	All Years
Law	5.0	14.5	19.6	13.6	7.2	12.0
Government	82.5	76.3	67.1	60.2	64.6	67.7
Business	5.0	3.9	11.3	19.3	19.2	13.9
Education	—	3.9	1.0	5.7	7.8	4.7

Note: For party eras, see table 1.

of the founding. Party era 3, the era of the Civil War and Reconstruction, is a transitional period between the founding and the progressive period. The progressive period takes on full bloom in party era 4. Party era 5 is the third skills epoch, that of big government. Table 18 presents the relevant data.

The data are not wholly supportive of the skills revolution concept, but there are hints at support. First, law, the generalist occupation, begins to be less important and education, a technocratic skill, begins to become more important in party era 5. So far, so good. Business, as predicted, becomes important in era 4 and stays important into era 5, instead of declining as expected. Lastly, government, especially important in the early eras, as expected, declines radically in importance with the onset of era 4 but does not rebound in era 5. These data are a bit too gross to test all the implications of the theory, though.

First, the government category combines both political and administrative skills. Table 19 refines this category into a number of more discrete types of government career. For present purposes, the major focus of attention is on the federal bureaucracy, and here one does see changes anticipated by the skills theory. Federal bureaucratic experience is unimportant in the early periods but begins to grow in importance in the transitional era 3 and in era 4. One must remember that the seeds of big government were sown in these eras with the beginnings of the regulatory state. By era 5 federal bureaucratic experience has become the second most important source of recruitment in the government category—only state and local government surpasses it.

TABLE 19
Major Government Career Before Appointment
(in percentages)

	Era 1	Era 2	Era 3	Era 4	Era 5	All Years
U.S. House	—	10.5	—	—	9.1	6.5
U.S. Senate	—	—	—	—	9.1	3.2
State/local govt.	76.9	73.7	80.0	62.5	40.1	74.2
Federal bureaucracy	7.7	5.3	20.0	25.0	36.4	22.6
Diplomatic corps	—	5.3	—	12.5	—	3.2
Judiciary[a]	15.4	5.3	—	—	4.5	6.5
(N)[b]	(13)	(19)	(10)	(8)	(22)	(62)

Note: For party eras, see table 1.
   a. Judiciary refers to all levels of government.
   b. The number of secretaries whose major career was in government.

One must remember, too, that lumped into the state and local category are some state bureaucrats, as well as executives and legislators. The addition of these bureaucrats would swell the ranks of bureaucrats even further. The only real deviation from the skills revolution sequence argued above rests with the continued importance of business as a major area of cabinet recruitment in party era 5.

One counter hypothesis to the skills revolution—cabinet transformation theory is the partisan alternation hypothesis. This hypothesis argues that the mix of precabinet occupations is a function of the rotation of parties in a competitive electoral system. In particular, one would expect Republican administrations to be more heavily loaded with recruits from the business than are Democratic administrations, and further, that Democratic administrations will recruit more heavily from the governmental category than will Republicans. The data in table 20 consider this hypothesis, and initial analysis suggests support for it. Democratic presidents recruit more heavily from the governmental category than do Republicans (by about 7 percent), and, more strikingly, Republicans recruit much more heavily from the business category than do Democrats (by over 11 percent). The three early parties show less variation.

TABLE 20
Primary Occupation by President's Party
(in percentages)

	Dem.	Repub.	Dem.-Repub.	Whig	Federalist
Law	33.3	26.6	10.7	29.4	7.1
Government	39.0	31.8	75.0	64.7	78.6
Business	22.6	34.1	10.7	5.9	14.3
Education	5.1	7.0	—	—	—

TABLE 21
Primary Occupation by President's Party and Party Era
(in percentages)

	Era 3		Era 4		Era 5	
	Dem.	Repub.	Dem.	Repub.	Dem.	Repub.
Law	41.9	30.8	55.0	32.8	31.4	17.5
Government	41.9	50.8	20.0	23.9	27.9	22.5
Business	9.7	15.4	20.0	38.8	33.7	46.2
Education	6.5	1.5	5.0	4.5	7.0	13.7

Note: For party eras, see table 1.

The data analysis has uncovered partial support for both the skills transformation and the partisan alternation hypotheses. Considering both simultaneously will reveal their comparative strengths, as well as any possible spuriousness. Table 21 breaks down primary occupation by both party and era for Democratic and Republican administrations in party eras 3, 4, and 5. The earlier eras and parties are excluded from the table because analysis revealed few party differences.

At first glance, the data in table 21 show some support for the partisan alternation hypothesis. Across the three party eras Democratic presidents recruit less than Republicans from the business category. Only in era 3 do Democrats recruit more than Republicans from the governmental category, a finding that is counter to the partisan hypothesis. The data are also supportive of the skills transformation hypothesis. Business recruitment steadily increases across both parties and eras. I would argue, in fact, that the secular skill transformations are stronger than the party differences because of this finding. That both parties responded by increasing recruitment from business testifies to the power of the secular skills transformation. And, though party differences are evident, the gap between Democratic and Republican recruitment from the business category narrows in era 5. These conclusions are similar to those of Prewitt and McAllister (1976). Though they found some support for party-based differences, they also found that secular forces impinging on both parties were even stronger.

These findings tell us something about the factors to which the cabinet responds and the mechanisms by which it does so. First, the cabinet has been resposive to broad secular forces that require or call for different types of secretaries. Such forces affect both parties. Second, the parties respond differently by emphasizing some occupational categories more than others. These differences are consistent with the ideological and electoral biases of the parties. Thus, the cabinet can be said to be somewhat electorally responsive. Lastly, the electoral responses do not appear as strong as the secular transformation forces. This may be due to the comparative strength of these two change factors or to the fact that, though the cabinet as an executive body is somewhat insulated from election concerns, as an administrative leadership it must respond to secular changes with the necessary skills. Comparative analysis of other institutions, such as the Congress, may help sort out which of these alternatives is correct.

Occupation and Exit Patterns

The previous section detailed the skill transformations of the cabinet, but one anomaly remains to be dealt with: the continued high levels of recruitment from the business category in party era 5. Though the progressive period saw increased recruitment from business, the rise of big government in era 5 need not signal a decline in that recruitment. Rather, the reason for recruitment from business in the period of big government may differ from that in the progressive period. Instead of recruiting for business-related management skills, as was the case in the progressive period, recruitment from the business category in the epoch of big government may indicate elements of interest group capture or liberalism (Lowi 1969). The large role of government in the economy may lure individuals from business into the government out of self-interest. In contrast is the supposed public-spirited motivation of business recruits in the progressive period. Two types of data on secretaries' careers, exit patterns and length of tenure, will help to test this hypothesis.

EXIT PATTERNS

Though the data at hand do not allow a definitive test of the interest group capture theory (Bernstein 1958), they do allow one to test some crucial implications of the theory. First, if the big government epoch is marked by capture or attempted capture, one should find increasing levels of exit into business after cabinet tenure is over, and length of tenure should vary by exit pattern. Table 22 considers the changing exit patterns across the five party eras.

First, the data indicate the professional nature of the early secretaries—they exited into other areas of the government at very high rates. As this trend decreased, two categories, law and business, show major increases. The increased frequency of exit into the legal category

TABLE 22

Exit Patterns

(in percentages)

	Era 1	Era 2	Era 3	Era 4	Era 5
Law	5.0	10.5	16.5	20.5	13.9
Government	60.0	57.9	47.4	35.2	38.5
Business	7.5	10.5	18.6	22.7	19.4
Education	2.5	1.3	7.2	6.8	6.8
Retirement	15.0	7.9	4.1	5.7	6.8
Death in office	7.5	6.6	3.1	4.5	4.1
Continuation in office or unknown	2.5	5.3	3.1	4.6	10.5

Note: For party eras, see table 1.

is in part a function of the increased recruitment of lawyers. Similarly the increased frequency of exit into the business category is probably a function of increased recruitment from it. Importantly for present purposes, there is no significant difference in the level of exit to business in party eras 3, 4, and 5.

To get a closer look at these exit patterns, one can compare them with recruitment patterns. The main point to emerge here is that there is a general tendency for exiting cabinet members to return to the category from which they were recruited. Table 23 and figure 1 show the relevant data.[4] Though this is not shown, this pattern of returning to one's category of recruitment remains stable across party eras.

LENGTH OF TENURE
Exit patterns do not help to distinguish the high levels of recruitment from the business category in party eras 4 and 5. It is not exceptional to find secretaries returning to the job categories from which they came. The secretariat, because of its dependence on presidential tenure, is in no way a career. With new presidents, especially if they are of the opposite party, the secretaries' tenure in office usually comes to an end. In fact, it is more likely that the secretary's tenure will end before the president's term has ceased.

However, variations in the tenure of secretaries may be an indication of the initial motivation to take the job and may thus bear on the question of interest group capture in era 5. One might hypothesize that governmental careerists will stay in the cabinet the longest, whereas those from business will remain in office for shorter periods. Further, those with self-interested reasons may stay in the cabinet for a shorter time than those motivated by duty and the opportunity for public service. The costs of cabinet service, the loss of income, the interruption of a business career, may be mighty tugs impelling secretaries to resume their nongovernmental careers. While calls to duty can become less insistent after imposing such a burdensome cost, they should immunize secretaries for slightly longer periods than those motivated by more pure forms of economic self-interest. Therefore, one may expect to find that the public-spirited business recruits of the progressive

TABLE 23

Exit and Recruitment Patterns

(in percentages)

Primary Occupation	Job Upon Exit or Exit Status						
	Law	Government	Business	Education	Retirement	Death in Office	Continuation in Office or Unknown
Law	63.1	24.4	13.2	25.0	15.6	36.8	26.5
Government	35.4	55.0	28.6	25.0	40.6	36.8	32.7
Business	—	15.0	54.9	31.3	37.5	26.3	32.7
Education	1.5	4.4	3.3	18.8	6.3	—	8.2
(N)	(65)	(180)	(91)	(32)	(32)	(19)	(49)

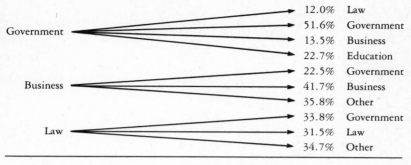

FIGURE 1
Primary Occupation and Exit Patterns

epoch serve somewhat longer than the more self-interested recruits of the big government epoch.

The data in table 24 strikingly confirm this hypothesis. To test this hypothesis most clearly, one must begin by making a distinction between a president's initial cabinet appointees and their replacements. The amount of time that a replacement can serve is constrained by the predecessor's length of service. Therefore, one will get a purer picture of the changing motivations by focusing only on initial appointees, as does table 24.

First, consider those recruited from the government as a control group. Their cabinet tenure increased from era 4 to era 5. Similarly, lawyers' tenure increased over the same two party eras. But the tenure of those recruited from business decreased from 56 months in era 4 to 49 months in era 5, a decline of 12.5 percent. Such a pattern is consistent with the hypothesized changing motivations of cabinet recruits from business.

Exit patterns, also presented in table 24, are similar. The tenure of lawyers does not alter, but that of secretaries who find other government jobs after leaving their cabinet positions increases from era 4 to era 5 by over 25 percent (45–61 months). However, the length of service of those exiting the cabinet to business decreases over these two

TABLE 24

Length of Tenure by Recruitment and Exit Patterns

(in months)

| | Recruitment | | | | | | Exit | | | | | |
	Era 1	Era 2	Era 3	Era 4	Era 5	All Years	Era 1	Era 2	Era 3	Era 4	Era 5	All Years
Law	—	30	34	39	54	40	64	27	32	42	43	37
Government	67	29	38	59	70	45	61	27	30	45	61	39
Business	34	38	41	56	49	49	—	41	47	71	52	55
Education	—	—	—	47	34	44	23	—	52	27	64	51
Retirement	—	—	—	—	—	—	117	48	48	24	69	64
Death in office	—	—	—	—	—	—	—	24	6	26	51	33

Note: Only initial appointees are included in the calculations. For party eras, see table 1.

periods by a staggering 27 percent (71–52 months). Again, these exit patterns suggest a change in motivation of those recruited from business or turning to it after their cabinet careers.

These findings have some implications for theories about skill transformations among political elites. Prewitt and McAllister (1976) lumped governmental and business administrative backgrounds together. This gives a picture of a transformation into one group primarily concerned with management of large governmental bodies. Certainly such a transformation has occurred, but governmental and business administrative skills are distinguishable and have different implications.

A governmentally trained administrative elite is probably more interested in a government career and in combining public service with career development. Those coming from or entering into business are more heavily oriented toward private gain. This is one interpretation of interest group capture theory, and a necessary ingredient for capture to occur is a large government, powerfully active in the economy, whose actions vitally affect the economic status of various sectors of the economy. Unnoticed by Prewitt and McAllister is the transformation of those recruited from business from one motivated by the ideals of scientific management and progressivism to one concerned with narrower economic self-interest. Though skills can be a useful barometer of a changing political elite, they must be placed within a larger context in order to understand their implications.

These findings also have implications for our larger themes of cabinet responsiveness and representativeness. These data seem to point to the permeability of the cabinet to interests in party era 5. Such a permeability is consistent with theories focusing on the growing role of interest groups in government since the rise of big government and interest group liberalism as a philosophy of government (Lowi 1969). Further, the rising importance of interest group representation in the cabinet may have profound policy consequences. For instance, interest group influence is often credited as a major source of disharmony among cabinet members and between them and the president. The increased role and impact of particular interests in the modern period may exacerbate such tendencies toward conflict.

Conclusions

The major topic of this chapter has been the intersection of the social bases of the cabinet and its representativeness. Four social background characteristics of secretaries were discussed: age, education, region, and occupation. For the most part we found the cabinet relatively representative of the nation in both symbolic and policy modes. One must temper this assessment, however, by noting the elitist nature of the cabinet. Secretaries as a group do not mirror the social characteristics of the population. Yet the cabinet has changed over the years in many of the same directions as the nation, for instance, by increasing educational levels and greater heterogeneity of region.

Perhaps the key point of this chapter is the demonstration of the cabinet's ability to respond to outside pressures, whether they emanate from long-term secular transformations or from electoral considerations. And response to both types of pressure ensures some level of symbolic representativeness associated with the forces promoting change. But perhaps as important, the cabinet's ability to change has policy implications as well. This is seen in the aging of the cabinet, its changing regional representation, and its occupational transformation. The first presents an indicator of the transformation from a revolutionary to a maintaining leadership. The second indicates the relative importance of regionally based policies and preferences in the executive council. The third indicates the growing importance of interest groups and the governmental bureaucracy for policy.

The cabinet can be seen as a representative and responsive body if one looks at the social background of secretaries. However, one must remember the limitations of the data presented thus far. First, few comparisons were made to other institutions. Hence we cannot say the cabinet is the most or least responsive and representative of bodies. Second, in some regards the cabinet showed little ability to respond. This was indicated in the discussion of education. The reasons for this somewhat limited ability to respond may derive from the elitist nature of the cabinet and the requirement for certain kinds of people to serve in it, no matter the nature of outside political and social pressures. Lastly, there are other dimensions of representativeness and responsiveness that must be considered. Succeeding chapters will do that job.

★ 4 ★

Party Politics

and the Cabinet

This chapter is concerned with the linkage between the political parties and the cabinet. This linkage has important implications for our discussion of the representative nature of the cabinet. Chapter 3 looked at representation from the vantage point of interest groups and social divisions. This chapter will look at representation from the vantage point of the parties, which can be said to cut across the divisions created by interests.

Political parties, like interest groups, evoke symbolic and policy representative concerns in the cabinet. For instance, the degree of partisanship of a cabinet may have important symbolic implications. A cabinet composed only of members of the president's party presents a different image to the public than a cabinet that mixes secretaries from within and without the president's party. Similarly, the partisan and bipartisan cabinet may differ in policies pursued. While the partisan cabinet may be most concerned with policies that will help party loyalists, the bipartisan cabinet may produce policies that are more national in scope. Thus, the kind of cabinet that a president constructs may be an important clue to his policy biases and those of his administration.

The degree of cabinet partisanship may also indicate the potential for teamwork in the cabinet. Though the British style of party and cabinet government does not describe how the U.S. cabinet functions, party politics in the United States do have major implications for the functioning of the U.S. cabinet. A partisan cabinet may be more easily forged into the president's team than the bipartisan cabinet. Within the councils of the cabinet, one may find less rancor and conflict if it has a strong partisan coloration than if it is a multicolored bipartisan cabinet.

However, partisanship of political leaders runs deeper than mere party label. Members of the same party may differ in their loyalty to and association with it. Secretaries vary in their level of precabinet party experience. Many have tended to be very active in party affairs and election campaigns, and some have either run for office or held some elective or appointive office before becoming cabinet officials. The discussion presented in this chapter will dig deeper than party label by looking at the secretaries' associations with and activities within their parties. This will give us a better sense of the partisan nature of the cabinet.

One factor with potential impact on the degree of cabinet partisanship is the nature of the party system. The parties have waxed and waned in strength over the course of U.S. history. If the cabinet is a repository of partisanship in the executive branch, one should detect temporal variation in cabinet partisanship that is consistent with theories of the rise and decline of parties. For instance, there has been considerable discussion about the decline of the parties in the United States (Burnham 1970). Does this decline show up in the cabinet as well? Similarly, Nelson Polsby (1978) argues that the changes in the presidential nomination system have loosened the ties between the president and his party, with the result that cabinet appointees are now less likely to be tied to important interests. Instead, they are more likely to be generalists and managers. Using more detailed information about cabinet career patterns, this chapter asks, Is Polsby's assertion correct?

These questions of cabinet partisanship, then, have important implications for our discussion of the symbolic and policy representative natures of the cabinet.

Party Membership and the Cabinet

It takes no statistical razzle-dazzle to find cabinet composition to be heavily biased toward the president's party. This point has been made in most studies of the cabinet, and most studies have felt the point so obvious that only a passing reference was necessary. The data in table 25 confirm this obvious point—presidents load their cabinets with members of their own party. (Recall that the secretary's party refers to allegiance at the time of appointment.) In all, 74.9 percent of all secretaries hold the same party affiliation as the president who appointed them. However, for about 10 percent party membership could not be ascertained. This is due to two factors. First, some of these secretaries are true independents; historical sources are notoriously poor at informing us if a secretary is an independent or not. Second, the historical record's incompleteness for some secretaries makes it impossible to detect if the secretary held a party affiliation or not. Thus, some data are truly missing here as well, and utilization of multiple biographical sources could not ascertain the party affiliation or the lack of it for this small subgroup of secretaries.

For all administrations there is a tendency to appoint from the president's party. Of the secretaries whose party affiliations we are certain of, 83.7 percent (74.9 percent of 89.5 percent) were members of the party of the president who appointed them. There is one interesting pattern of note, however: membership of the president's party is less crucial for appointment for the early parties than for the later Democratic and Republican parties. For the three early parties, the Federalists, Democratic-Republicans, and Whigs, only 50–57 percent of the secretaries were of the president's party. For the two modern parties the figures are 78 percent for the Democrats and 80 percent for the Republicans.

This old-modern party difference suggests that we may more finely disaggregate these data by time. Table 25 presents these data broken down by party era as well. Within eras, presidential preferences for members of their own party are again revealed. Further, there rarely are interparty differences within party eras. The one exception is era 2,

TABLE 25
Congruence of Political Party by Party Era
(in percentages)

Secretary's Party	President's Party					
	Dem.	Repub.	Dem.-Repub.	Whig	Federalist	All
Same as president's	78.0	80.2	50.0	55.9	57.1	74.9
Different from president's	10.7	10.8	42.9	35.3	7.1	14.6
None or unknown	11.3	9.0	7.1	8.8	35.7	10.5
Era 1						
Same as president's	—	—	50.0	—	57.1	53.8
Different from president's	—	—	42.9	—	7.1	30.8
None or unknown	—	—	7.1	—	35.8	15.4
Era 2						
Same as president's	87.8	—	—	55.9	—	77.5
Different from president's	9.8	—	—	35.3	—	16.9
None or unknown	2.4	—	—	8.8	—	5.6
Era 3						
Same as president's	70.0	83.0	—	—	—	78.1
Different from president's	23.3	12.3	—	—	—	16.7
None or unknown	6.7	4.7	—	—	—	5.2
Era 4						
Same as president's	73.7	82.1	—	—	—	79.3
Different from president's	15.8	7.4	—	—	—	10.3
None or unknown	10.5	10.5	—	—	—	10.5
Era 5						
Same as president's	76.7	78.2	—	—	—	77.0
Different from president's	5.8	10.2	—	—	—	8.5
None or unknown	17.5	11.6	—	—	—	14.5

Note: For party eras, see table 1.

where Democratic presidents appoint about 30 percent more secretaries from their own party than do Whig presidents. Still, Whig presidents recruit the majority of their secretaries from the Whig party, though, as with the earlier Democratic-Republicans, a large minority is recruited from other parties.

These figures indicate a growing maturation of the party system, which, in the early decades of the Republic, was more fluid than now. Parties developed and were replaced by new ones. Yet, as the party system settled into a stable pattern of Democratic and Republican competition, cabinet recruitment rigidified, and membership in the president's party became almost a requisite for the job. In these initial data, then, one can observe the development of the party system from a fluid system, where loyalty to party is of only modest importance, to a stable system, where it is desired among members of the cabinet.

The Political Activity of Secretaries

Mere party labels do not tell one much about the political experiences of the secretaries, though. The labels do not indicate the varying experiences that the secretaries have had with the parties, their degree of involvement, or their loyalty. Perhaps more telling would be to investigate the quality of the relationship of the secretaries to the parties.

This investigation begins with a coding from the biographical record of seven activities that were adapted from Kemp's study of regulatory commissioners (1983, 390). The variables are whether or not the secretary:

held an elective or appointive office (OFFICE);
ran for office (CANDIDACY);
held a party office (PARTY OFFICE);
worked in a presidential campaign (PRESIDENTIAL CAM-
PAIGN);
was appointed by the president for whom the secretary campaigned (APPOINTMENT):
held a position in a state or local campaign organization (STATE
CAMPAIGN);

was officially involved in candidate fund-raising (FUND-
RAISING).

Most of these activities are clear, but a few words need to be said
about some. First, APPOINTMENT (names of variables are in capitals
in the list) is not a separable activity of a secretary but is a subset of
PRESIDENTIAL CAMPAIGN. As such it represents a form of presidential patronage. Second, holding a party office (PARTY OFFICE)
could include attendance at a national nominating convention as a
delegate but could also include county chairmanship, national head-
quarters assignments, and other party-related activities.

One important point about these variables is their conservative nature. If no mention of the activity was made in the biography, the
secretary was coded as not having performed the activity. Surely, the
short biographies will overlook some political activities, especially
when the activity is informal. The coding allows only formal activities.
The degree of informal activity will be missed in these data. The formal
mention requirement raises the threshold of what constitutes political
activity. Thus, these data probably understate the political activity of
secretaries.

Table 26 reports the distribution of political activity on the part of
secretaries. Compared to the general public, cabinet members are politically highly active. Almost three-quarters have held some elective or
appointive office, and over half have run for office. By no means are
these people newcomers to politics. As a group, they are also heavily
involved in more direct party matters. Over one-quarter have held some
party post, while smaller numbers have worked in campaigns at either
the national or state and local levels, or have worked as fund-raisers.
One cannot overlook the high levels of political activism of secretaries
before their cabinet service.

The sheer amount of data presented by this list of activities is somewhat unwieldy for analytic purposes, but data reduction—that is, scaling techniques—can help to clarify the picture of secretarial activity.
First, inspection of the activity distribution may lead one to hypothesize that there are easier and harder activities. With such a hypothesis,
on the basis of actual performance, holding an office (OFFICE) would

TABLE 26
Politcal Activity Scale
(in percentages)

OFFICE	74.6
CANDIDACY	57.5
PARTY OFFICE	27.4
PRESIDENTIAL CAMPAIGN	8.3
APPOINTMENT	6.4
STATE CAMPAIGN	5.1
FUND-RAISING	3.0

	Guttman Scale Results	
	7 Variable Model	5 Variable Model
CR	.937	.952
Minimum marginal reproducibility	.831	.900
CS	.624	.523

Note: OFFICE—held an elective or appointive office;
CANDIDACY—was a candidate for elective office;
PARTY OFFICE—held a state or local party office;
PRESIDENTIAL CAMPAIGN—worked in a presidential election campaign;
APPOINTMENT—was appointed by the president for whom he or she campaigned;
STATE CAMPAIGN—worked in a state or local election campaign;
FUND-RAISING—helped in fund-raising.

be easiest, followed by running for office (CANDIDACY) and so on until one comes to the hardest activity, fund-raising. Further, if there are easier and harder activities, one can also hypothesize that secretaries who perform the harder ones will also perform the easier ones. This is the logic of Guttman scaling.

The seven items were subjected to Guttman scaling, and results are presented in table 26. The coefficient of reproducibility of .937, the minimum marginal reproducibility of .831, and the coefficient of scalability of .624 all indicate relatively strong Guttman properties, but inspection of the Yule's Q intercorrelations (see table 27) reveals some anomalies. The major problems revolve around two variables,

TABLE 27
Yule's Q Intercorrelations of Political Activity Measures

	Yule's Q Intercorrelations					
	2	3	4	5	6	7
1. OFFICE	.93	.32	−.08	−.20	.14	−.08
2. CANDIDACY		.40	−.08	−.23	−.16	−.01
3. PARTY OFFICE			.70	.63	.88	.89
4. PRESIDENTIAL CAMPAIGN				.95	.61	.81
5. APPOINTMENT					.38	.62
6. STATE CAMPAIGN						.85
7. FUND-RAISING						

Note: For codes, see table 26.

OFFICE and CANDIDACY, which are negatively related to most of the others. This would indicate a lack of association to the other variables. Also, though not shown, these two variables exhibit relatively large numbers of classification errors when subjected to the Guttman scaling. With essentially dummy variables, it is often easy to build what appear to be strong Guttman scales. Other diagnostics are required to understand the properties of the data more fully.

Factor analysis may prove valuable under such circumstances. The seven variables were factor analysed using a nonrotated varimax solution. The results are presented in table 28. The factor results support the suspicions based upon the Yule's Q intercorrelations. First, two factors were uncovered. Both have strong eigenvalues: 1.36 and 1.23 respectively. An eigenvalue of greater than one usually indicates an identifiable factor. Second, the factor loadings indicate that OFFICE and CANDIDACY form one factor (factor 2), whereas the other variables load strongly on factor 1. These results seem to indicate two separate types of activity, those related to running or holding an office, and those others that are more strongly associated with party or campaign organizations. Holding or running for an office may be done in a nonpartisan atmosphere, and the thresholds for those activities are often low. The more difficult party and campaign activities may have higher

TABLE 28
Factor Analysis of Political Activity Measures

	Factor 1	Factor 2
OFFICE	.11	.65
CANDIDACY	.15	.85
PARTY OFFICE	.49	.14
PRESIDENTIAL CAMPAIGN	.70	−.17
APPOINTMENT	.59	−.21
STATE CAMPAIGN	.36	−.02
FUND-RAISING	.36	−.04
Eigenvalue	1.36	1.23
% of variance explained	43.6	39.6

Note: For codes, see table 26.

entry barriers, such as the requirement of a party organization or the technical skills necessary to work in fund-raising.

This leads to a threefold classification scheme that will be used for most of the subsequent analysis. First are the nonactives. These people have neither worked in campaigns nor held or run for office. At a higher level of activity are the officeholders and candidates. Let us label them the governmental actives. At a still higher threshold of activity are the organizational partisans, who may have run for and held office but, more importantly, have worked for the party organizations in some campaign or organizational capacity. Let us label them the organizational actives. An organizational active who has never held or run for office may be the archetypal backroom political boss.

Table 29 shows the relationship between governmental and organizational activity. First, 18.4 percent of the secretaries are nonactives. Second, 76.9 percent had previously either run for office or been appointed or elected to an office. Third, 31.6 percent were engaged in one or more organizational activities. Not surprisingly, though, the overwhelming percentage of those who were organizationally active were also governmentally active (126 of 148, or 85.1 percent). Still, there is a small group of organizational actives without any of the two

TABLE 29
Governmental and Organizational Activity
(in percentages)

Government Activity	Organizational Activity	
	One or More	None
One or more	26.9	50.0
(N)	(126)	(234)
None	4.7	18.4
(N)	(22)	(86)

governmental forms of activity. To use some terminology from Verba and Nie's study of political participation (1972), there are considerable numbers of specialists, but still some 26.9 percent (126 of 468) of the secretaries are complete actives; that is, they have performed both governmental and organizational activities.

Classifying the secretaries into one of three categories, and noting that most of the organizational actives are also governmentally active, produces a distribution of 18.4 percent who are inactive, 50.0 percent who are only governmentally active, and 31.6 percent who are only organizationally active.

Recruitment Category

A number of questions arise as to the sources of variation in the political activity of the secretaries. One initial place to look is the category from which they were recruited. For instance, one would expect that, just by the nature of the job, those recruited from primary jobs in government would be heavily represented among the governmental actives. Just by definition, many of those from the government category were appointed to their jobs. Similarly, the nature of the job would lead one to suggest that very few inactives will be found in the group from the government category. For instance, there will be some who moved up the ranks of the civil service and do not owe their jobs to election or appointment (and thus would not be coded as having ever held a political or governmental job because of appointment or election), but the number should be small.

Similarly, the general nature of law and the view of law as a training ground for a political career would lead one to expect large numbers of lawyers involved in some aspect of politics, either governmental or organizational, or both. Like those from the government category, there will be few lawyers who are politically inactive.

The other two categories, education and business, will differ from government and law. Both education and business should display large numbers of inactives. Further, the general nonpartisan bias of the education category should lead to the hypothesis that few educators will have experience in party organization.

Data in support of these hypotheses are presented in table 30. Recruits from the government category are by far the most active, and the bulk of their activity, as hypothesized, is in the governmental, not organizational arena. Lawyers are the second most active group, and more of them are governmentally active than are organizationally active. However, lawyers are the most organizationally active, even though the differences between them and recruits from government and business are very small.

Recruits from business are only modestly active when compared to lawyers or governmental recruits. Over one-third of secretaries who come from business backgrounds are inactive, according to the activity scale. Still, nearly two-thirds are active, and they are equally divided

TABLE 30
Political Activity by Recruitment Pattern
(in percentages)

	Law	Government	Business	Education
Nonactives	14.6	4.7	37.5	54.2
Governmental actives	48.5	61.5	32.5	37.5
Organizational actives	36.9	33.9	30.0	8.3

between the two forms of activity. The lower levels of governmental activity among business recruits, when compared to the governmental activists and lawyers, may indicate a general unwillingness on the part of the public to vote for people in business. It may also indicate an inhibition on the part of executives about appointing them to governmental posts, perhaps because of possible conflict of interest. Viewed from another angle, though, the data indicate relatively high levels of political activity by recruits from business.

Secretaries from the education category are the least politically active. Over one-half are inactive. Further, educators rarely get involved in partisan organizational politics, a finding that indicates that the hypothesized nonpartisan bias of the academia and nonprofit private foundations may be the case. Yet educators are willing to become involved in government. Much of this may come from their greater wilingness to accept appointive jobs as opposed to elective ones.

Party Differences

Political activity of secretaries may also vary by political party. For instance, theories of the rise and decline of the parties suggest that party organizational strength has varied over the years (Chambers and Burnham 1975). The activity data presented here may be taken as measures of the organizational vitality of one important leadership group of the major parties.

Considerable party differences are evident in the activity data (table 31). The early parties show low levels of organizational activity, a finding that makes sense when one remembers that they were developing the party organizations that one now recognizes (Chambers and Burnham 1975). For the later parties, one finds more modest differences. Republican secretaries are slightly more likely than Democrats to possess party organization experience, but Republicans are also more likely to be nonactives. This finding concurs with our image of the Republican party as more organizationally developed and coherent than the Democratic party (Gibson et al. 1983), but also more dependent on those with little political experience to serve as candidates, especially in areas where the Republican party has been historically weak (Fishel 1973).

TABLE 31
Political Activity by Secretary's Party
(in percentages)

	Dem.	Repub.	Dem.-Repub.	Whig	Federalist
Nonactives	11.2	21.8	—	6.9	11.1
Governmental actives	55.9	35.6	90.5	69.0	88.9
Organizational actives	32.9	42.6	9.5	24.1	—

Interparty differences are modest not only when one compares the party allegiances of the cabinet members, but also when one looks at the types of secretary appointed by presidents of the different parties (see table 32). Again one finds low levels of organizational experience for secretaries of the early presidents. This reflects the lack of opportunity for organizational activity given the nature of the party organizations at that time. Also, the same modern party differences that were noted above recur. Democratic presidents are less likely to appoint secretaries without either governmental or organizational experience and also slightly less likely to appoint those with organizational experience. The similarity of these findings with those of the previous paragraph is due to the strong bias for presidents to appoint secretaries of their own party.

One may wonder, though, if presidents will be cautious in appointing opposition party members to their cabinets, and if people strongly tied to their parties will be adverse to accepting appointment in a cabinet of an opposition president. Both lines of argument suggest that one will find very few opposition party cabinet members with histories of organizational activity.

The data presented in table 33 support the hypothesis. Presidents are much less likely to appoint opposition party members with strong organizational ties. The data indicate only 13 such cases. Such a finding confirms the validity of the activity variable as being able to measure the organizational ties of secretaries to their parties. The analysis also looked at the behavior of presidents of the different parties and came to the same conclusion—presidents appoint few opposition party mem-

TABLE 32
Political Activity by President's Party
(in percentages)

	Dem.	Repub.	Dem.-Repub.	Whig	Federalist
Nonactives	17.5	24.3	3.6	—	14.3
Governmental actives	47.5	38.8	89.3	76.5	85.7
Organizational actives	30.5	36.9	7.1	23.5	—

TABLE 33
Political Activity by Political Party
(in percentages)

	Secretary's Party	
	Same as President's	Different from President's
Nonactives	15.7	11.8
Governmental actives	46.2	69.1
Organizational actives	38.2	19.1

bers with organizational background (for Democratic presidents the *N* is 6; for Republicans the *N* is 4). The data, though, cannot tell one if the motivation behind this bias is presidential caution or inhibition on the part of prospective appointees. Probably both are at work.

The Cabinet and the Party Eras

The above analysis presented data on the political activism of cabinet secretaries. Findings were consistent with expectations regarding activity and political party and with activity and opposition party membership. The activity data appear valid, at least for the broad sorts of comparison offered here. These data may also help us chart the rise and decline of the party organization, a topic that has been much discussed in recent years (e.g., Key 1955; Clubb, Flanigan, and Zingale 1980;

Burnham 1970). If the activity data relate to the parties as these theories of party change suggest, we may be able to say some things about the ability of the cabinet to represent the parties in this high-level council.

In recent years there has been a veritable flood of studies concerning the U.S. party systems, most revolving around the concepts of critical elections (Key 1955; Clubb, Flanigan, and Zingale 1980), realignments (Burnham 1970), and dealignments (Norpoth and Rusk 1982). These studies have categorized the party systems into five eras, roughly corresponding to the following periods: 1789–1824, 1825–60, 1861–96, 1897–1932, 1933 through the present (though there is some confusion as to the number of party systems in the last period, and whether the dealignment years of post-1964 should count as a separate party system era; see the discussion in chapter 3).

The bulk of the party system studies have focused on electoral politics and the voting behavior of the public, but a number have also looked at changes in state and national legislatures (Clubb, Flanigan, and Zingale 1980) and the judiciary (Funston 1975) across these periods. The analysis presented here differs from the literature to date in two important ways. First, the focus is on the national executive. Second, I accept the notion of the party eras, but instead of trying to demarcate the changes from one era to another, or the causes of the changes, I will look at how the cabinet has changed across the five party eras.

Two important characteristics of the party eras theoretically motivate the present analysis. One is the changing relationship of the national executive parties to the state and local parties. The second is the degree of organizational vitality and integrity of the parties in the different party eras. How reflective is the cabinet of the party systems? The answer to this question sheds much light on the nature of state-national relations and the degree of integration of the parties, as well as the role of the national executive branch in the life of the parties.

The literature on the party systems provides one with a portrait of the parties at different times that serves as a benchmark for analysis. The two characteristics of local-national relationships and the degree of organizational development paint the portrait.

First, consider the changing nature of state-national party relations. In the first party era, that of the Federalists and the Democratic-Republicans, ties between the national and the state and local parties were relatively weak. This was primarily a function of the youth of the parties and the generally paramount position of the state governments when compared to the national government (Young 1966). Those who came to Washington, especially to serve in the Congress, stayed for short periods and often returned to the then more important state governments.

Over three-quarters of the cabinet members in party era 1 were recruited from the ranks of state and local government. However, unlike congressmen and senators, who returned frequently to the state-house, few secretaries returned to state government after their cabinet tenure (table 34). Of these early secretaries who remained in government after their cabinet service ended, only 8.3 percent returned to the states or localities upon exit from the cabinet, yet 66.7 percent remained in the federal government as legislators, federal executives (including the president and vice president), and/or diplomats. (Of those in the judiciary category, some are federal, but the coding did not separate nonfederal from federal appointments. Had I done so, the percentage in the federal branch would have increased).

TABLE 34

Exit Careers in Government

(in percentages)

Exit Career	Era 1	Era 2	Era 3	Era 4	Era 5
U.S. House	0.0	9.8	2.4	0.0	0.0
U.S. Senate	12.5	29.3	29.3	16.7	12.5
State/local government	8.3	12.2	7.3	6.7	6.3
Federal bureaucracy	25.0	12.2	19.5	33.3	28.1
Presidency	12.5	7.3	2.4	3.3	0.0
Vice-presidency	4.2	0.0	0.0	0.0	3.1
Diplomatic corps	12.5	14.6	19.5	16.7	28.1
Judiciary	25.0	14.6	19.5	23.3	21.9
(N)	(24)	(41)	(41)	(30)	(32)

Note: For party eras, see table 1.

Though the state and national parties were never fully integrated, the degree of integration increased with the development of the parties. For many years, it was the custom to talk in reference to each major party, of the existence of as many "parties" as there were states, and a national party existed only for the nomination and election of the president once every four years. Beginning with party era 2, and continuing until the end of era 4, the federal nature of the party system, not its national component, was paramount. Hints of this pattern are found in these cabinet data as well. Again, state and local governments served as the prime source of recruitment into the cabinet (table 19), but, beginning in era 4, a decline in such recruitment can be observed. This was due to the increased recruitment from the national government categories and the general increase of recruitment from business (with the concomitant decline in overall recruitment from the government categories). Still, as with cabinet officers of era 1, exit into state and local government never served as a major postcabinet career option. The national government, especially the federal bureaucracy, the diplomatic corps, and increasingly the upper legislative chamber, became the new homes of ex-secretaries who intended staying on in the government. (The figures for exit into the national government, excluding the judiciary, are: 73.2 percent for era 2; 73.1 percent for era 3; and 70.0 percent for era 4. These percentages represent only those who stayed in the government.)

Thus far, these data indicate two important facts, the dominance of the states and localities for recruitment to the cabinet, but of the national government for exit from it. This is similar to the Polsby argument of the professionalization of Congress (1968), except that cabinet officers stayed in the national government in some capacity from the beginning of the nation. In this sense, at least in the executive branch, the national government was supreme in the career hierarchy of government personnel, a transformation that would come only many years later to the legislative branch. Yet, as in the legislative branch, recruitment from state and local government indicates at least a one-way direction of integration of the local and national parties.

Party era 5 is in many ways the most complex. Whereas the second half of the era witnessed major dealignment in the public, some studies have indicated an increased nationalization of the parties and more vigorous and healthy national parties as the period progressed (Gibson et al. 1983). These nationalizing tendencies are apparent in these data as well. First, recruitment from state and local government dropped off precipitately, with recruitment from the federal bureaucracy and, interestingly, from the Congress, increasing in importance. This is the first period of major cabinet recruitment from the Congress. Here I must parenthetically remind the reader that I am speaking only about the primary careers of secretaries. If one were to use the looser definition of any congressional experience, then one would find decreasing rates. Davidson (1969, 64) cites the following figures for cabinet members with any congressional experience: 1795–1832, 67 percent; 1861–96, 37 percent; 1897–1940, 19 percent; 1941–63, 15 percent (Davidson does not provide figures for 1833–60). However, for my purposes, primary career is a more useful construct in understanding career paths, as chapter 3 explained.

Yet, while recruitment from the Congress increased, exit into the Congress, though still important, decreased. The earlier patterns of exit into the national government, however, remained high (71.8 percent). These data emphasize the nationalization of the cabinet in the period of the nationalization of the parties.

These data tell a story of federal-local party relations that fits well with interpretations of the locus of party power across the party eras, but they do not shed much light on the changing organizational maturity of the parties across the same periods. The activity data presented earlier in the chapter can reveal much about the organizational vitality of the parties, though.

Party era 1 is known as a period of developing party organizations, but not developed organizations. Organizational development proceeded rapidly, and the late 1800s and early 1900s were the heyday of the party bosses, who epitomized the party as well-organized electoral machines. A number of factors, however, began to undermine these organizationally strong parties. First, the development of the new mass communications media, first radio, but especially television, decreased reliance on party workers to inform voters and get out the vote. Second, the nationalization of the government, especially its welfare functions, supplanted the parties as dispensers of private benefits. And lastly, the nationalization of the nomination processes decreased the power of local bosses as they were replaced by pollsters, advertising professionals, and issue-motivated amateurs.

The activity measure developed in this chapter provides useful information on the vitality of party organizations. Table 35 presents the data.

An inspection of two elements of the organizational dimension, holding a party office and working in a presidential campaign, proves instructive. The first measures to some degree the state party experiences of cabinet officials. Though more than just state and local offices may be included here, only a very few secretaries held national party office, and of those who did, most held state party office as well. This indicator shows a pattern resembling the historical pattern offered above.

Party era 1 shows few secretaries holding party office, primarily because of the lack of such posts. Well-developed party organizations with formal positions were only beginning to come into existence as era 1 came to an end. Growth in the number of secretaries holding such positions increased from 5.0 percent in era 1 to 18.4 percent in era 2, and reached a high of 41.2 percent in era 3. Beginning in era 4, a decline in the number of secretaries with prior experience in party posts begins, though is still high at 30.7 percent. This decline continues into era 5, when only 26.9 percent held party posts. The pattern presented

TABLE 35
Political Activity by Party Era
(in percentages)

	Era 1	Era 2	Era 3	Era 4	Era 5	All Years
Nonactives	7.5	2.6	9.3	23.9	30.5	18.4
Governmental actives	85.0	72.4	45.4	43.2	35.3	49.1
Organizational actives	7.5	25.0	28.9	19.1	37.5	32.5
Party officeholders	5.0	18.4	41.2	30.7	26.9	27.4
Presidential campaign workers	0.0	6.6	10.3	5.7	11.4	8.3

Note: For party eras, see table 1.

here resembles Burnham's argument that the decline of the parties began after the election of 1896 and the conclusion of party era 3. If the cabinet reflects the nature of the party system, as I argue it does, then this is added evidence that the decline of the parties as organizations began about the turn of the century and continues to the present.

Consistent with Burnham's argument of party decline is the thesis of nationalization of the parties. The nationalization of the parties helped to weaken local and regional party units and their ties to the national party structures. Further, advances in communications technology decreased the need for masses of party workers, thereby lessening the dependence of candidates for national office on local party leaders and bosses, the people who commanded the armies of party workers. Television proved a more efficient method of transmitting messages from candidates to voters, and it was direct—mediation by party workers of varying ability and quality was no longer needed. This line of argument suggests that, as the state and local party organizations declined, experience in national organizations, especially presidential election campaigns, would become more important.

Table 35 presents data on this point, but they are inconclusive. Whereas presidential campaign experience was absent in party era 1 because of the method of presidential selection, slight growth appeared in era 2, as expected. And as expected, era 5 shows the largest percentage of secretaries who have worked on presidential campaigns. But the percentage of presidential campaign participants in era 3 is almost as high as in era 5, and it contrasts sharply with the much lower levels of eras 2 and 4. In any event, the number of secretaries with presidential campaign experience is relatively small throughout the history of the nation.

The decline of the party organizations in presidential cabinet politics can be seen in other data presented in table 35. The percentage of nonactives increases across the five eras to a high of 30.5 percent in era 5, except for a drop in era 2. The era 2 drop reverses in era 3, and the long-term trend continues. Though the percentage of organizational actives increases strongly in era 5, one must remember the numerous types of activity counted in that measure. The more striking point for the party decline theory is the increase of nonactives in the cabinet. In all, the data support Burnham's party decline theory, though short-term influences on the process are evident as well.

Party Differences Within Eras

Though the theories of party decline and party systems do not offer much guidance in terms of party differences within eras (most variations assume organizational similarities), there is good reason to raise the question of such differences. Conventional and historical impressions of the parties lead to some differences relevant to the subject at hand.

First of all, the Federalist party existed in an era before the establishment of well-organized parties. Therefore, it is not likely that Federalist secretaries would possess much experience in the party organizations. On the other hand, one tends to think of the Democratic party as the party of the urban boss. This does some injustice to the urban base of the Republican party prior to the New Deal, but it is a view worth testing. Tables 36 and 37 consider these differences from the perspective of the secretary's party and the appointing president's party, respectively.

Within eras, one notices some party differences, though they are not huge. First, as expected, Federalist secretaries posses no party organization experience. (See table 36). Though the Democratic-Republicans of Jefferson show some organizational experience in party era 1, one should read such numbers with caution because of the small Ns involved.[1]

However, by era 2 both Whigs and Democrats show similar levels of party organizational experience. These levels climb to a high point in era 3, when almost half of both Democratic and Republican secretaries had some experience in their party's organizations.

Era 4 shows continued high levels of organizational experience, though the figures begin to decline from the highs registered in the previous period. Now Democrats display somewhat greater organizational experience. There seems to be a great influx of nonactives among Republican secretaries, which may indicate a linkage between Republicans and business, with the resulting recruitment of these political amateurs because of these close ties.

TABLE 36
Political Activity by Secretary's Party and Party Era
(in percentages)

		DemRepub.	Federalist
Era 1	Nonactives	0.0	12.5
	Governmental actives	90.5	87.5
	Organizational actives	9.5	0.0
		Dem.	Whig
Era 2	Nonactives	4.4	4.3
	Governmental actives	75.6	69.6
	Organizational actives	20.0	26.1
		Dem.	Repub.
Era 3	Nonactives	0.0	8.2
	Governmental actives	52.0	42.6
	Organizational actives	48.0	49.2
		Dem.	Repub.
Era 4	Nonactives	5.3	20.7
	Governmental actives	52.6	44.8
	Organizational actives	42.1	34.5
		Dem.	Repub.
Era 5	Nonactives	20.0	36.4
	Governmental actives	44.0	19.7
	Organizational actives	36.0	43.9

Note: For party eras, see table 1.

Major differences are also evident in party era 5. Republicans finally begin to show more organizational experience than Democrats, perhaps due to the strengthening of the national Republican party in the latter half of this period. But Republicans also are highly inactive. In fact, nonactives become the second largest group among Republicans in this era. Democrats also show increases in nonactives among cabinet officers, but the numbers pale when compared to the Republicans.

The patterns for presidents and their cabinets is similar to the story of the preceding paragraph. Whereas the cabinets of presidents of different parties within party eras are very similar, the differences between Democrats and Republicans in eras 4 and 5 stand out (see table 37). In era 4, Democratic presidents recruit more from the ranks of the organizationally active than do Republicans, though Republicans recruit more nonactives. However, presidents of both parties show similar levels of recruitment of governmental actives.

In era 5 recruitment of the organizationally active reaches parity between the parties, mostly because of a decline of such recruitment by Democrats. However, presidents of both parties increase their level of recruitment from the nonactives by about 10 percent. These trends also indicate that Democratic presidents recruit governmental actives more

TABLE 37
Political Activity by President's Party and Party Era
(in percentages)

		Dem.-Repub.	Federalist
Era 1	Nonactives	0.0	7.7
	Governmental actives	95.0	92.3
	Organizational actives	5.0	0.0
		Dem.	Whig
Era 2	Nonactives	4.8	0.0
	Governmental actives	70.7	80.0
	Organizational actives	24.4	20.0
		Dem.	Repub.
Era 3	Nonactives	6.6	9.2
	Governmental actives	46.7	46.2
	Organizational actives	46.7	44.6
		Dem.	Repub.
Era 4	Nonactives	15.8	25.4
	Governmental actives	42.1	43.3
	Organizational actives	42.1	31.3
		Dem.	Repub.
Era 5	Nonactives	26.7	35.0
	Governmental actives	40.7	28.7
	Organizational actives	32.6	36.2

Note: For party eras, see table 1.

than do Republicans, and that Republicans register slight increases in organizational actives but healthy increases of nonactives. Perhaps the strong ties of business to the Republican party leads Republicans to recruit more heavily from the ranks of the nonactives. Other analysis hints at the importance of business people and their general lack of organizational experience, in the Republican party. However, these party differences should not be blown out of proportion—secular trends and party eras have more impact than interparty differences on organizational experience.

The Implications of the Parties for the Cabinet

The previous sections have documented the historical relationship between the parties and the cabinet. In general, the parties in the cabinet rise and fall in importance as historical models of the rise and decline of the parties suggests. However, this importance has other notable implications that relate to presidential control of the cabinet, harmony within it, and length of service.

First, presidents seek greater control of their cabinets as their administrations age, or so a number of scholars argue (Polsby 1978; Best 1981; King and Riddlesberger, 1984). They may accomplish this by replacing initial appointees, who are often strongly tied to interest groups, with people more loyal to the president. Loyalty to party may increase loyalty to the president. Party loyalists may view themselves as members of a team in the cabinet, whereas interest group secretaries may view themselves as spokespersons in the cabinet for that interest. Do initial appointees and replacement appointees differ in terms of secretarial-presidential party congruence, as suggested?

Second, if party increases loyalty to the president, if it increases a spirit of team membership, will it motivate secretaries to stay in the cabinet longer? Can party loyalty increase cooperation among secretaries and help them overcome differences and personal ambitions for the sake of the party and the party's leader, the president? If party does not have these expected impacts, it would be difficult to view the cabinet as being able to represent the interests of the parties.

Initial and Replacement Appointees

A number of scholars have remarked on the cyclical nature of president-cabinet relations. Presidents seem to begin their terms in office optimistic about their working relations with their cabinet members. However, as time progresses and departmentalism and incremental budgeting forces set in, strain develops in the relationships between the president and his secretaries and among the secretaries (Cronin 1980). Probably the classic example of the deterioration of president-cabinet relations is the Carter administration, which began with a close relationship, only to undergo a sweeping reshuffling and mass firing of secretaries midway through the presidency. This deteriorating relationship would lead one to expect presidents to replace initial appointees with people who would be more congenial to the president, more amenable to presidential direction, and/or more loyal (Polsby 1978; Best 1981; King and Riddlesperger 1984).

One way to reduce president-cabinet discord is to replace initial appointees of the opposition party with those from the president's party, who may be more loyal to the president. Hence, they may be more likely to go along with the president when the strains associated with departmentalism and interest group pressures set in. One type of "president's man" on the cabinet, therefore, may be the "party man."[2]

Before proceeding, one must discuss the distinction between initial and replacement appointees. For presidents elected in their own right, the distinction poses no problem. However, for those who acceded to the office because of the death or resignation of the previous incumbent, one must decide who the true initial appointees of the succeeding president are. Are they the carryovers from the previous administration, or are they the first appointees who replaced those of the previous president? Both definitions cause problems. Carryovers might not be the successor president's true choice. However, some of them serve for such a long period of time that they become the successor president's true choice.

The coding rules used here combine elements of both. If the carryover serves more than a year into the successor president's administration, he or she is considered the replacement president's initial appointee. Any new appointment made within one year of the accession to office of the new president is also considered an initial appointee. This one-year period allows for the transition, during which the new president is given time to claim the office fully and the memory of the old president (the one elected to office) is allowed to fade.

Table 38 considers the possibility that initial appointees from the opposition party will be replaced by members of the president's party, but the data do not support this expectation. For four of five presidential parties, there are more replacement appointees than initial appointees from the opposition party than from the president's own party. Most of these percentage differences are small, however, and therefore should not be focused upon too strongly. The important point, though, is that presidents do not see partisanship as a solution to disharmony between themselves and their cabinets.

However, sheer party name is not a sensitive measure of party loyalty. Following the argument presented thus far, one may more critically assess party loyalty by looking at the types of experience the secretaries have had with the parties. Table 39 compares the types of political experience of initial and replacement cabinet members.

The first thing to note from the table is the almost identical levels of political activity of the initial and replacement appointees. Such a comparison may be masking party differences, so the next columns of the table indicate whether or not the secretaries were of the president's party, as well as whether they were initial or replacement appointees. As I noted before, like initial appointees, replacements come disproportionately from the president's own party. Surprisingly, replacements from the president's party do not differ much from initial appointees of the president's party. And, though initial appointees from the opposition party were less likely to have broad organizational experience, replacements from the opposition party were somewhat more likely to have organizational experience than initial appointees from the opposition party. Further analysis looked at each presidential party separately and again found no significant differences in political activity of initial and replacement cabinet appointees. Again, as I argued earlier, presidents do not seem to view partisanship or degree of partisanship as a solution to president-cabinet discord.

TABLE 38

Secretary's Party by President's Party and Appointment Status

(in percentages)

	Dem.		Repub.		Dem.-Repub.		Whig		Federalist	
	I	R	I	R	I	R	I	R	I	R
Same as president's	81.4	74.7	79.8	80.6	40.0	44.4	76.9	42.9	20.0	77.7
Different from president's	8.1	13.2	10.5	11.1	40.0	44.4	23.1	42.9	20.0	0.0
Unknown	10.5	12.1	9.6	8.3	20.0	11.1	—	14.3	60.0	22.2
(N)	(86)	(91)	(104)	(108)	(10)	(18)	(13)	(21)	(5)	(9)

Note: I = Initial appointee

R = replacement appointee

TABLE 39

Political Activity by Appointment Status and Political Party
(in percentages)

	All		Same as President's		Different from President's	
	I	R	I	R	I	R
Nonactives	18.6	20.7	12.9	18.4	15.4	9.5
Governmental actives	47.5	48.1	47.1	45.8	73.1	66.7
Organizational actives	34.6	31.2	40.0	35.8	11.5	23.8

Note: I = Initial appointees
      R = Replacement appointees

These findings clearly display the limits of party impact on the cabinet. Whereas earlier sections showed the historical relationship between the parties and the cabinet, these findings suggest limits to the strength of the parties. The diverse nature of the parties may be part of the reason why presidents do not seek party members more as replacement secretaries. Diversity may not promote the policy cohesion that presidents seek. To create cabinet harmony, presidents may have to rely more on personal than party loyalty. Such a theme of the limits of party in the United States is not unknown to scholars of the party system.

Party Activity and Cabinet Service

Though presidents do not seem to view partisan manipulation of their cabinets as a road to a more harmonious and presidentially directed cabinet, partisanship may affect a secretary's orientation toward the cabinet. One point noted throughout this study is the cost of cabinet service. Such a cost, coupled with the impossibility of making a career of the cabinet, puts great pressures on secretaries to retire from the cabinet, often into the more lucrative business world. Do party ties extend cabinet service?

The working thesis here resembles the one proposed in the last section: cabinet members of the president's party, and especially those with strong party attachments, will view their cabinet service not only as service to the president, but also as service to the party. Hence, loyalty to the party (and to the president) may delay a secretary's exit from the cabinet. Like analysis on length of service in the previous chapter, this section analyzes only initial cabinet appointments. Replacements are constrained in service by the length of service of the original appointee. Therefore, length of service of replacements does not measure purely how long such secretaries desired to stay in office.

Table 40 presents the relevant data for this analysis. Consider the first column in the table. All initial appointees served on the average for 44.5 months (or about 3 years and 8½ months). Secretaries of the president's party served somewhat longer than the average (47.4 months), whereas those from the opposition party served considerably less (33.2 months). Thus, initial analysis supports the contention that party membership affects length of service.

However, as I have argued previously, party affiliation is a notoriously crude measure of party loyalty. The party activity data presented above are better at measuring loyalty. Does loyalty extend service, as I hypothesized?

Reading across the top row in table 40 indicates that nonactives are more prone to remain in the cabinet than governmental or organizational actives, with those of the last group staying longer than the governmental actives. But for these numbers to make sense, they must be disaggregated by party. Again, one finds that nonactives of the

TABLE 40
Length of Tenure by Political Activity and Party
(in months)

	All Initial Appointees	Secretary's Party		
		Same as President's	Different from President's	None or No Information
All	44.5	47.4	33.2	39.7
Nonactives	54.0	68.0	25.5	49.6
Governmental actives	41.9	45.1	21.3	39.2
Organizational actives	44.5	46.7	66.0	15.3

president's party stay much longer than either governmental actives or organizational actives. The difference is quite large, too (68.0 months for inactives, 45.1 for governmental actives, 46.7 for organizational actives). And while organizational actives stay longer than governmental actives, they do so by only 1.6 months, surely a trivial margin. One must emphasize, though, that presidents appoint few nonactives from their own party to their initial cabinets.

As for the opposition, organizational actives stay much longer than nonactives or governmental actives, but again the numbers are so small that one should not make much of this point. Activity seems to have an impact, but counter to our expectations—the lack of previous political activity actually increases cabinet tenure.

It could be that inactives appointed to the cabinet are more flattered than those with more experience, and therefore they want to stay on longer. It is possible that nonactives are appointed because of their loyalties to the president, while party people are appointed for political reasons, such as representation of important interests in the party, interests that may collide with presidential policy. And, one must not forget, these patterns may be driven by presidential preferences, not secretarial ones. However, attribution of cause is difficult to assess because of limitations of the data. Lastly, the Ns of party inactives are so small as to mitigate against a detailed analysis of their exit patterns.

The results just presented are equivocal. Though party membership increases cabinet tenure, previous party-related political experiences do not seem to support the hypothesis under investigation. And reasons why organizational activity does not work in favor of longer cabinet tenure are not apparent or easily tested with the data at hand. Again, personal loyalty to the president may be the key. The diffuse nature of the parties in the United States, their geographic divisions, and their ties to numerous and often conflicting interests all frustrate the construction of cohesive parties. Thus, presidents may have to rely more on personal loyalty than party loyalty when building and attempting to maintain their cabinets.

Still, the overriding conclusion is that party membership may reduce the potential for tension or disagreement with the president or otherwise reduce the costs of cabinet membership. However divided and decentralized the U.S. parties are, divisions between the competing parties may run even deeper.

Conclusions

Clearly, party politics are relevant to the cabinet, but there are important limits to their injection into the cabinet. First, cabinet-party ties tightened and loosened much as the strength of the parties waxed and waned in U.S. history. When the parties were stronger, secretaries were more involved in party politics before their cabinet service. When the party institutions weakened, fewer secretaries were found to have been active in party affairs. The parties may serve as important gate-keepers in the recruitment of cabinet personnel, but only when they also serve as developers and promoters of political talent. When the parties do not provide the politically talented and motivated with the opportunity to hone their skills, learn their trade, and exercise their ambition, these people will seek other avenues to promote their political careers.

However important the parties may be in recruiting cabinet secretaries, they decline in importance once the secretaries are in office. Party and party loyalty seem to have little impact on the president's choice for replacement appointees and on the secretary's decision to stay or leave the cabinet.

Both the conclusions of the previous paragraph and the findings of chapter 3 point to interest groups as having a more prominent place in cabinet politics. In a sense this is just a restatement of the competition between parties and interest groups for influence in U.S. politics. However, the pat and neat answer that interest groups are more influential—that is, that they are better represented than the more diffuse, decentralized, and divided parties—requires qualification, for the proposition is not so simple.

In part, research on parties and the cabinet has been neglected because of the assumption of the dominance of interest groups. The proliferation of cabinet departments is one sign of the power of interests. Further, the oft noted conflict between president and secretary is usually blamed on the power of interests both within a department and over the secretary. Hence the famous line from Harding's budget director, Charles Dawes, "The members of the cabinet are a president's natural enemies" (cited in Neustadt 1960, 39).[3]

The data presented in this and the previous chapter, however, may modify the interest group dominance argument. First, most of the studies claiming that interest groups are especially influential in the cabinet were written in the period of relatively weak parties and strong interests, party era 5 (Cronin 1980; Fenno 1959; Polsby 1978). Data presented here show that party ties to the cabinet declined from era 3 to era 5 and that interest group ties to the cabinet may have increased from era 4 to era 5. Recall the thesis of the impact of big government on interests and the changing motivation to serve in the cabinet on the part of recruits from business over the last two party eras.

It may be the case, though data here are not definitive, that the relative impacts of party and interest group influences on the cabinet have varied across the party eras as well. For instance, in era 3, when party ties to the cabinet were at their zenith and interest group ties were less apparent than now, party influence may have been greater than is generally observed today. It may even be the case that parties were more important than interests, and that cabinet politics more closely resembled party government than at any other time. Such thoughts are speculative but consistent with the data. However, data on what transpired at cabinet meetings and on conflict between presidents and their secretaries are needed to test these hunches.

These thoughts reveal complex relationships among the cabinet, political parties, and interest groups that have implications for our concerns with representation. A key element to representation is responsiveness. However, responsiveness is not something that may come from charity, guilt, or altruism. The base for responsive behavior may lie in the incentive system structuring the representative's environment.

Though cabinet members do not have to run for office, political pressures may still be brought to bear. Political party pressures are in part internalized through learning from and association with the parties, but also in part through the ability of the parties to create an environment of team spirit. Other than stacking the cabinet with members of the same party, little team spirit seems to exhibit itself in the councils of the cabinet.

Interest group pressures may become entrenched within departments and therefore have an impact on the secretary. But not all departments are "controlled" by single interests; some, like Housing and Urban Development and Health and Human Services, have ties to numerous, often competing, interests. And during earlier times, currently powerful interests (for example, Agriculture) did not have departmental representation in the cabinet.

To speak of the cabinet in terms of interest group capture or of party government is to speak of types of symbolic and policy representation. Though it is clear that interests are indeed important, parties compete with them. Interest and party representation may vary historically, and by department. Chapter 5 deals with the question of departmental variability and representational problems.

★ 5 ★

The Secretaries

and the Departments

To coin a phrase, not all cabinet departments were created equal. From this it follows that not all cabinet members are equal. Departments differ in the time and circumstances of their creation, their budget and personnel levels, and their ranking in the presidential succession order. Secretaries differ not only as individuals, but also in their level of prestige, their political power, and their access and importance to the president.

Cronin has summarized these differences into a distinction between the "inner" and "outer" cabinets (1980, 276–86). The idea of an inner and outer cabinet is not new. Fenno often mentions such a distinction (1959, 117–19). Nor is the distinction unique to the United States. British scholars have also remarked on a distinction that closely resembles Cronin's (Herman and Alt 1975, xviii, xxi–xxii; Daadler, in Herman and Alt 1975, 252). But it is Cronin who has spent the most time developing the concept.

Basically, Cronin argues that there are two cabinets, an inner cabinet and an outer cabinet. These can be viewed like concentric circles around the president, with the inner cabinet the smaller ring and the outer cabinet the larger one. The inner cabinet is therefore closer to the president than the outer cabinet. The member departments of the inner cabinet are the departments of State, Treasury, and Defense (War and

Navy) and Justice. The other departments compose the outer cabinet. The inner cabinet departments comprised George Washington's original cabinet.

According to Cronin, the inner cabinet positions are "vested with high-priority responsibilities that bring their occupants into close and collaborative relationships with presidents" (1980, 276–77). One may even go so far as to argue that these high-priority functions are those that no government, no matter how limited and laissez-faire, could do without. Part of the importance of these departments is seen in the Nixon reorganization proposals, which would have kept these departments in tact, while merging the others (cited in Cronin, 278).

Further, the outer cabinet departments are plagued by strong interests that pull the secretary away from the president. The creation of many of the outer departments can be seen as governmental responses to strong economic interests—Agriculture, Interior, Labor, and Commerce, for instance. Strong interests in the outer departments often mean that they and their secretaries are not well insulated from nonpresidential political pressures, such as those coming from the Congress, state and local governments, and interest groups. The interest advocacy role of secretaries of the outer departments often places them at odds with the White House, and such conflict often leads to isolation and restricted access to the president (Cronin 1980, 285–86).

This conceptual distinction between departments is based in part on a theory of access and the forces that promote or hinder access to the president. The inner cabinet departments are considered "closer" to the president, both in the concentric circle configuration and in a policy sense. This distinction also implies an informal organization among the departments that contradicts the structure of the cabinet according to its organizational chart, where departments are viewed as equals save for their position in the presidential succession hierarchy. When informal organization departs from the organizational chart, it is often because the organizational chart does not represent power relationships realistically.

In this sense, then, the distinction between inner and outer cabinet departments is also a distinction between the more and less powerful departments. The more powerful are the ones granted easier access to the president. These access differentials can be viewed as the cabinet's accommodation to different political forces and/or groups, primarily national versus local or special interest concerns.

The inner-outer cabinet distinction also helps solve a representational problem at this high level of the executive: which is to be represented better, national interests or more special interests. The inner departments represent national problems—defense, foreign relations, the economy—where special interest concerns, though not without importance, are often considered as somewhat less important. Inner cabinet prominence is the way that the cabinet and the president ensure that national interests dominate when conflict between national and special interests occurs.

The inner-outer distinction, then, relates to our focus on representation and the two types considered most pertinent to the cabinet, symbolic and policy representation. The concentric circle geography symbolically places the inner cabinet closer to the president than the outer cabinet. Similarly, this spatial distinction suggests that policies emanating from the president and cabinet will be more nationally biased than would be the case if all departments were equal in the eyes of the president and the secretaries. Lastly, if the distinction holds under empirical scrutiny, then we have a basis to suggest the greater potential responsiveness of the cabinet to the inner than the outer departments. However, the tests to follow will determine only the usefulness of the inner-outer distinction, not the degree of representativeness or responsiveness. Other kinds of data are necessary to answer those questions.

While Cronin has spelled out an important conceptual distinction, one that is rooted in the nature of the departments' responsibilities and the plural nature of society and politics in the United States, there has been little empirical testing of his conceptual scheme. Evidence for it is almost solely anecdotal. The only empirical test to date is offered by Weisberg (1980), who applies ambition theory to transfers of secretaries among the departments but finds only modest support for the conceptual distinction. The aim of this chapter is to build upon and refine Cronin's theory and derive some testable propositions about distinctions among the departments.

Specifying Differences among Departments

Cronin's discussion leads to a focus on three factors that may distinguish among the departments. The first relates to the recruitment process; the second to the appointee's closeness to the president; and the third to implications for running the departments. These three factors represent the mechanics and processes associated with the distinction between the inner and outer cabinets.

Recruitment Patterns

One may infer from Cronin that there may be crucial differences in the recruitment patterns of secretaries of the inner and outer departments. One factor that makes inner secretaries important to a president is the special expertise that they bring to the job. For instance, one can expect to find the secretaries of state and defense possessing considerable experience in government. Also, the importance of law to the attorney general's job and economics to the treasury secretary's job should lead one to expect an attorney general with a legal background and a treasury secretary with a financial background. On the other hand, the outer cabinet departments are often considered the domains of vested interests. Therefore, it would not be shocking to find those secretaries recruited from the ranks of those important interests.

At this point it is probably useful to make another distinction, that between the older and newer outer cabinet departments. The older departments are Interior, Agriculture, Commerce, and Labor, and the newer ones include Housing and Urban Development, Health, Education, and Welfare/Health and Human Services, Education, Energy, Transportation. In his study of cabinet transfers, Weisberg (1980) found the distinction to be useful. One important difference between these two types of outer cabinet department is that the older ones tend to have environments that are dominated by one strong interest. In contrast, the newer ones have more complex environments that may be composed of many, often conflicting, interests. Throughout the analysis I make use of this distinction, which, I will show, is quite useful at times.

Before proceeding, a note about the analysis is in order. Prior to the Civil War, only two outer cabinet departments, the Postmaster General's Office and the Interior Department, existed, and there is some ambiguity about placing the former with the other outer departments. The later addition of the other outer departments transformed the nature of the cabinet and led to the status differences discussed in this chapter. The early, pre–Civil War cabinets, composed almost entirely of inner cabinet departments, may not be wholly comparable to the cabinets of the post-1860 period. Thus, the analysis to follow excludes the pre–Civil War from calculations. (Initial analysis sometimes found this to make a difference. Tables with figures for 1789–1984 are provided in the Appendix.)

The expectations mentioned above can be measured, albeit indirectly, with our background data. First, consider the legal bias expected for the attorney general. One way to measure this expectation is to use the measure of primary occupation prior to cabinet appointment, which was discussed in chapter 3. Table 41 presents the relevant data. Clearly, there is support for the idea of recruiting the attorney general from the legal profession. While the primary occupation measure is crude (many with legal training were not primarily employed as lawyers), attorneys general were more heavily recruited from these ranks than all other cabinet secretaries. While 30.3 percent of all secretaries since 1861 were primarily employed as lawyers, 61.4 percent of attorneys general were so employed.[1] Further, the Justice Department leads all other departments in recruitment from the legal profession. Fenno (1959, 70) and Mann and Smith (1981, 224) confirm this finding and also report that attorneys general have all been trained in the law.

There is also some evidence, though weaker than the case for the Justice Department, that shows the importance of governmental experience to the State Department and the defense departments. It should be through government, more than the other categories, that one develops knowledge and expertise about foreign and defense affairs. Whereas 31.1 percent of all secretaries since 1861 were recruited from the government category, 44.4 percent of the secretaries of state, 32.3 percent of secretaries of war, and 32.0 percent of secretaries of the navy were recruited from the government category. Though these figures

TABLE 41
Primary Occupation by Department, 1861–1984
(in percentages)

	Law	Government	Business	Education	N
State	40.7	44.4	11.1	3.7	27
Treasury	17.9	35.9	43.6	0.0	39
War	45.2	32.3	22.6	0.0	31
Justice	61.4	34.1	0.0	4.5	44
Navy	32.0	32.0	36.0	0.0	25
Defense	18.2	18.2	54.5	9.1	11
Postmaster	20.5	33.3	35.9	10.3	39
Interior	38.2	32.4	26.5	2.9	34
Agriculture	17.4	26.1	39.1	17.4	23
Commerce and Labor	25.0	50.0	25.0	0.0	4
Commerce	4.5	4.5	81.8	9.0	22
Labor	11.8	11.8	52.9	23.6	17
HEW	8.3	50.0	16.7	25.0	12
HUD	50.0	25.0	12.5	12.5	8
Transportation	37.5	25.0	37.5	0.0	8
Energy	0.0	0.0	100.0	0.0	3
HHS	0.0	100.0	0.0	0.0	2
Education	0.0	50.0	0.0	50.0	2

Note: HEW: Health, Education, and Welfare;
HUD: Housing and Urban Development;
HHS: Health and Human Services.

weakly support the hypothesis, the 1789–1984 figures do so more strongly—all, 41.0 percent; War, 50.9 percent; State, 63.4 percent; Navy, 45.6 percent. Again, other studies concur with this finding (Fenno 1959, 75; Mann and Doig 1965, 32; Mann and Smith 1981, 221).

Other departments, especially Treasury and Post Office, also showed heavy rates of recruitment from the government, but the nature of the government service of these cabinet members differs slightly. Postmasters general usually found their government/political experience in the political parties, especially in the early years. Remember, the government category as operationalized here includes party positions as well as formal government posts. Historically, postmasters general are likely to have more party experience than the secretary of state, whose experience lies more with actual and bureaucratic governmental service. This point is documented with data on the political experience of the secretaries as reported in table 42.

The defense secretary's background does not conform to expectations, though. Most defense secretaries are recruited from business (see also Mann and Doig 1965, 32 and Mann and Smith 1981, 221). This represents quite a change from the War Department secretaries, who came more heavily from the government category. The change may be accounted for by the increasing size of the Defense Department after World War II as compared to the peacetime size of the defense establishment prior to that war. Management techniques, especially those of large corporations, became increasingly important in the postwar years to running the Defense Department. This is most evident in the case of Robert McNamara, Kennedy's defense secretary, who brought management techniques to Defense and was instrumental in developing the planning-programming-budgeting systems in the department. Though the suggestion is speculative, this recruitment change may also measure the maturing relationship between Defense and its private sector contractors, so often termed the military-industrial complex. Though these data are not a strong test of that theory and all of its policy implications, they are surely consistent with it.

The background data may also allow indirect measurement of the interest group ties of outer cabinet department secretaries. A handful of departments stand out as examples of interest group departments; Commerce, Agriculture, Labor, Interior, and Education.

The nature of the Commerce Department would lead one to expect heavy recruitment from the ranks of business and finance. Commerce is, after all, the department charged with promoting the private sector. The findings are among the clearest in this regard. A whopping 81.8 percent (see table 41) of the commerce secretaries were recruited from the business category, the overwhelming majority from the ranks of corporations and other large enterprises. Other studies also find this sector link (Mann and Doig 1965, 54; Mann and Smith 1981, 223–

TABLE 42

Previous Political Experience, 1789–1984

(in percentages)

	Party Office	Candidacy	Office	State Campaign	Presidential Campaign	Fund-Raising	Appoint-ment
State	22.2	51.9	80.8	0.0	9.5	0.0	6.7
Treasury	33.3	51.3	71.1	8.8	8.8	0.0	14.8
War	29.0	61.3	80.0	0.0	10.7	4.8	10.5
Justice	34.1	50.0	82.9	10.0	19.4	3.6	18.5
Navy	28.0	68.0	68.0	4.0	12.5	0.0	12.5
Defense	18.2	27.3	54.5	0.0	9.1	0.0	0.0
Postmaster	59.0	43.6	70.3	13.8	24.1	12.5	21.7
Interior	44.1	70.6	90.0	3.0	9.4	5.3	15.8
Agriculture	17.4	52.2	60.9	4.3	0.0	0.0	0.0
Commerce and Labor	25.0	0.0	100.0	0.0	0.0	0.0	0.0
Commerce	27.3	13.6	45.5	4.6	0.0	9.1	0.0
Labor	5.9	11.8	29.4	0.0	5.9	0.0	0.0
HEW	25.4	41.7	75.0	16.7	16.7	16.7	8.3
HUD	12.5	12.5	37.5	12.5	0.0	0.0	0.0
Transportation	25.0	50.0	62.5	12.5	25.0	25.0	12.5
Energy	0.0	33.3	66.7	66.7	0.0	0.0	0.0
HHS	100.0	50.0	100.0	50.0	0.0	0.0	0.0
Education	0.0	0.0	50.0	0.0	0.0	0.0	0.0

Note: Party office—held a state or local party office;
  Candidacy—was a candidate for elective office;
  Office—held an elective or appointive office;
  State campaign—worked in a state or local election campaign;
  Presidential campaign—worked in a presidential election campaign;
  Fund-raising—helped in fund-raising;
  Appointment—was appointed by the president for whom he or she
    campaigned. For abbreviations, see table 41.

24). Further, since 1960 only two commerce secretaries, Elliot Richardson and Juanita Kreps, did not have experience in the management of a large business enterprise.

The Labor Department has been considered the major base of union and labor influence in the government, and it would come as no sur-

prise to find union representation crucially important in the recruitment of labor secretaries. Evidence does not find strong direct ties to
labor, though. For instance, in the period from 1913 through the
Eisenhower administration, Fenno found that Republican presidents
appointed all their labor secretaries from the leadership of unions, but
that Democrats did not name any union officials to that post (1959,
75). In the period from 1960 through 1981, Mann and Smith found
that only two of six Republican appointees and one of three Democratic
appointees came from labor's ranks (1981, 224).

Though direct union representation may not be common, indirect
representation of labor interests can be measured. First, table 43 indicates that over half of the labor secretaries came from the East, the
region where labor is most powerful (along with the Midwest). Slightly
less than half of all secretaries came from the East. Admittedly, this is a
most crude indicator of labor representation. The most that one can say
is that the regional representation of labor secretaries does not contra-
dict the point about group representation offered here.

Also, there is some evidence of interest representation in the Agriculture department. My measures are again somewhat crude and indirect,
but 56.5 percent of the secretaries of agriculture came from the Midwest, the prime agricultural region of the nation throughout most of its
history, whereas about 30 percent of all secretaries since 1861 came
from that region. Further, other studies (Fenno 1959, 72; Mann and
Doig 1965, 48; Mann and Smith 1981, 223) confirm the midwestern
and agricultural bias among secretaries of this department.

A fourth department considered a key base for select interests is
Interior. Interests here are concerned with development of land, min-
eral rights, and water, for example. The region of the country most
concerned with these interests is the West, and secondarily, the Midwest. And one finds overrepresentation of westerners and midwesterners among the ranks of interior secretaries since 1861 (32.4 percent
from the West and 52.9 percent from the Midwest, compared to
national rates of 10.3 percent and 31.1 percent respectively). Again,
other studies confirm this finding (Fenno 1959, 72; Mann and Doig
1965, 48; Mann and Smith 1981, 223).

For these old-line departments, then, one can find ties to interest

TABLE 43
Region of Origin by Department, 1861–1984
(in percentages)

	East	South	Midwest	West
State	59.3	7.4	18.5	0.0
Treasury	48.7	10.3	35.9	0.0
War	41.9	9.7	35.3	3.2
Justice	54.5	13.6	22.7	9.1
Navy	52.0	16.0	20.0	4.0
Defense	50.0	0.0	40.0	10.0
Postmaster	38.5	15.4	43.6	2.6
Interior	5.9	5.9	52.9	32.4
Agriculture	26.1	0.0	56.5	17.4
Commerce and Labor	50.0	0.0	25.0	25.0
Commerce	54.5	18.2	22.7	4.5
Labor	53.8	15.4	15.4	15.4
HEW	40.0	20.0	20.0	20.0
HUD	42.9	14.3	28.6	14.3
Transportation	42.9	14.3	0.0	42.9
Energy	0.0	66.7	0.0	33.3
HHS	100.0	0.0	0.0	0.0
Education	0.0	50.0	0.0	50.0

Note: For abbreviations, see table 41.

groups that fit with our understanding of these departments. The newer, social departments generally do not exhibit such a neat and tidy interest group relationship because they often have had to deal with numerous interests that sometimes are in conflict. Of the newer departments, only Education can be said to be an interest department like the four mentioned above, and though there have been only two education secretaries, one has had long experience in education, but too much should be made of an N of 2.

On the whole, the recruitment pattern for the newer departments shows no single path. Of the 35 secretaries of the 6 departments (Health, Education, and Welfare, Health and Human Services, Education, Energy, Housing and Urban Development, and Transportation)

13 (37.1 percent) came primarily from government, 8 (22.9 percent) came from law, 9 (25.7 percent) came from business, and 5 (14.3 percent) came from education. Occupationally, there is no dominant pattern. Regionally, there is also a good mix: 39 percent are from the East, 19.4 percent are from the South, 12.9 percent are from the Midwest, and 29.0 percent are from the West. If anything, the West is overrepresented among these departments, but this may reflect its growing electoral importance in recent years and the relative youth of these departments.

A second recruitment pattern suggested by Cronin relates to the degree of partisan association of the secretaries of the different departments. Other than Justice, the inner cabinet departments, in Cronin's words "preside over policies that usually . . . are perceived to be largely nonpartisan or bipartisan. . . . The domestic departments almost always are subject to intense crossfire between partisan and intense interest groups" (1980, 283). Thus, one may expect to find greater degrees of partisan association among the outer cabinet departments than among the inner ones.

Table 44 begins the analysis by displaying the degree of congruence between the secretary's and the appointing president's party. At first inspection, there is some support for the greater partisanship of the outer cabinet and the lesser partisanship of the inner cabinet. All of the older outer departments were headed by secretaries of the president's party about 70 percent of the time. Similarly, all of the newer outer departments save Education were headed by secretaries of the president's party at least 75 percent of the time. For the inner departments, the story is slightly different, for the percentages of secretaries from the president's party do not quite match those of the outer departments, though some of the inner ones exhibit strong partisanship.

One finds that 76.8 percent of the secretaries of inner cabinet departments since 1861, including the attorneys general, were appointed by presidents of the same party. In contrast, the figures for the older and newer outer departments are 81.9 percent and 82.9 percent, respectively.[2]

These data, though consistent with Cronin's theory, provide only a weak test. Party affiliation says little about the degree of partisanship of

TABLE 44

Congruence of Political Party by Department, 1861–1984

(in percentages)

	Secretary's Party		
	Same as President's	Different from President's	Unknown
State	73.1	23.1	3.8
Treasury	79.5	12.9	7.6
War	64.5	16.1	19.4
Justice	75.0	20.5	4.5
Navy	88.0	12.0	0.0
Defense	90.9	0.0	9.1
Postmaster	84.6	7.7	7.7
Interior	84.8	9.1	16.1
Agriculture	69.6	4.3	26.1
Commerce and Labor	75.0	25.0	0.0
Commerce	72.7	13.6	13.6
Labor	52.9	5.9	23.5
HEW	91.7	0.0	8.3
HUD	87.5	0.0	12.5
Transportation	75.0	0.0	25.0
Energy	100.0	0.0	0.0
HHS	100.0	0.0	0.0
Education	0.0	0.0	100.0

Note: For abbreviations, see table 41.

the secretary. More instructive would be to look at party organizational activities. To be consistent with Cronin, one would hypothesize that secretaries in the inner cabinet departments, though affiliated with the president's party, will not be as involved in party affairs as those of the other departments.

Some initial data have been presented in table 42, which displays the political activities of the secretaries. More useful than this wealth of data is the typology of activity presented in chapter 4 (organizational actives, governmental actives, and nonactives). For present purposes, the organizationally active category is most instructive and shows whether a secretary: held a party office; held a position in a state or local campaign; worked in a campaign for a presidential candidate; held a position in fund-raising; or was appointed by the president for whom the secretary campaigned. Table 45 presents data on the organizational activities of the secretaries of the president's party by department.

Comparing across departments, these data do not seem consistent with the Cronin contention. Not only do secretaries from two inner cabinet departments rank high in organizational activity (Justice and Treasury), but there is wide variance in organizational activity among all three types of cabinet department. However, averaging across the

TABLE 45

Organizational Actives in President's Party by Department,
1861–1984

(in percentages)

State	26.3
Treasury	48.4
War	35.0
Justice	54.5
Navy	31.8
Defense	30.0
Postmaster	66.7
Interior	46.4
Agriculture	25.0
Commerce and Labor	33.3
Commerce	37.5
Labor	16.7
HEW	36.4
HUD	14.3
Transportation	66.7
Energy	66.7
HHS	100.0
Education	0.0

Note: An organizational active did at least one of the following: held a position in a state or local party organization; worked in a state or local campaign; worked in a presidential campaign; was a fund-raiser. For abbreviations, see table 41.

three types of department reveals the greater involvement of secretaries of outer cabinet departments than those of inner departments in party organizational politics, though these differences are weak at best. Of the inner secretaries since 1861, 40.4 percent engaged in at least one party organizational activity. The figures for the older and newer outer departments are 44.0 percent and 44.8 percent, respectively.

Still, one must mention the great departmental variability in organizational activity within the three departmental groupings. As expected, attorneys general are highly involved in party affairs, but one also finds this to be the case for treasury secretaries. Perhaps, considering the great party differences in economic policy and the role of treasury in developing and implementing that policy, one must rethink Cronin's "nonpartisan or bipartisan" characterization of that department.

Similarly, secretaries of agriculture and labor showed little inclination toward party organizational activity. For Labor this may be explained by the general reluctance of labor movement officials to take formal positions in the parties (though they have certainly been very active in campaigning for candidates). Agriculture is more of a mystery, but strong farmer interest group pressure may push recruitment more toward those active with the farm groups than the party groups. This is not so surprising, either, considering the high levels of political activity of farmers and farm groups outside traditional party politics (Anderson et al. 1984).

On the whole, the data generally support Cronin's inner-outer distinction, though the party-related data are not always overwhelming or strong. The recruitment patterns for the inner cabinet departments generally conformed to expectations, as did those for the interest group departments. Further, the newer outer departments displayed no dominant recruitment pattern, a finding that is in line with the diverse nature of the interest environments of these departments. More importantly, as the theory would predict, recruitment of both the older and newer outer departments differed significantly from the pattern of recruitment of the inner departments. At the same time, recruitment patterns as related to the parties also held up, though the organizational activity data were only weakly supportive.

Ties to the President

One important thread in Cronin's discussion of inner and outer cabinet departments, recruitment, has been tested, and generally supported. A second factor that Cronin discusses and/or implies relates to the ties of the secretaries of the different types of department to the president.

Cronin argues that inner cabinet officers have "close personal friendship(s) . . . with the president" (1980, 282). The reliance upon friends in the inner cabinet is due to the counseling nature of those departments. Whereas outer department secretaries are viewed as interest representatives, inner department secretaries are viewed as presidential advisors who are important in the development of key aspects of the president's program. Further, the importance of the policy areas governed by these departments requires secretaries whom the president can trust, and if or when disagreements present themselves, they will be loyal enough to go along with the president rather than their own departmental or personal feelings. Friendship prior to the president's and the secretary's term in office may help bond the secretary to the president and help the president trust and rely upon the secretary.

It is difficult to get a solid handle on friendship and trust from biographical data of the sort used in this study, but there are pieces of data that can help test these notions indirectly and should at least discriminate among inner and outer cabinet departments in the ways predicted by Cronin's theory.

Congruence of state of origin of presidents and secretaries may be used as an indicator of previous president-secretary relationships. One may argue that presidents come to office with a local, and not a national, base and that they rely quite heavily on friends and supporters from their home state. It is quite likely that these supporters began their association with the president long before he entered national politics. Thus, one should find presidents placing more home state supporters in inner cabinet departments than in the two types of outer department.

While not conclusive, the data in table 46 support this view: 13 percent of inner cabinet officers since 1861 came from the president's home state; in contrast, only 7.1 percent of the older outer cabinet and

TABLE 46

**Congruence of Secretary's and President's Home State,
1861–1984**

(in percentages)

State	14.8
Treasury	20.5
War	6.5
Justice	15.9
Navy	8.0
Defense	0.0
Postmaster	15.4
Interior	2.9
Agriculture	4.3
Commerce and Labor	50.0
Commerce	13.6
Labor	5.9
HEW	16.7
HUD	0.0
Transportation	12.5
Energy	0.0
HHS	0.0
Education	0.0

Note: For abbreviations, see table 41.

8.6 percent of the newer outer cabinet hailed from the president's home state.[3]

Other data collected are more sensitive to these pretenure ties. One of the organizational activity measures recorded whether the president for whom a secretary campaigned also appointed that secretary to office. These data are presented in table 42. First, one should remove the postmaster general from calculations involving the outer cabinet. Traditionally, this post has been reserved for party leaders, and often the national party chair also held this post. Thus, the department is different, in this sense, from the other outer departments, though one cannot call it an inner department. The data are quite clear on this point about the postal department. It leads all of the other departments in most of the party-related activities, especially the one related to presidential appointment.

The data in table 42 are clear on the point of presidents appointing more inner than outer department secretaries to office who campaigned for them. Of the inner department secretaries since 1861, 7.9 percent had this tie to the president compared to only 3.8 percent of the outer department secretaries. When one breaks down the outer cabinet departments into older and newer, the figures become 3.0 percent and 5.7 percent respectively. Again, these results are less than definitive, and the differences are small, but when one considers the crudeness of the regional variable and the small Ns involved in the campaigning-appointment variable, that one should find any relationships at all is heartening and leads one to feel that there is merit in Cronin's point about president-secretary ties. Testing the ties argument is difficult, though, because of the lack of easily accessible data.

Implications for Managing the Departments

In Cronin's distinction of cabinet departments are implications for secretary's management of the department and behavior while in office. Cronin and others argue that the outer cabinet departments are more subject to interest group pressures, which serve to pull the secretary's loyalty in two directions, toward the department and toward the president. Thus, outer department secretaries should find themselves in more conflict than those of inner departments with the president.

Further, the impact of the interests in the outer cabinet may limit or curtail a secretary's management of the department. Lower-level personnel may be more attuned to the clientele groups that the department (or agency or bureau) serves than to the secretary (and, by implication, the president). One may then find outer department secretaries facing more conflict or resistance to presidential and departmental policies than inner department secretaries. Management difficulties for secretaries of the newer outer departments may be exacerbated further by the complexity of the department's interest group environment. The newer outer departments often serve multiple interests, and secretaries may find not only the expected patterns of resistance of lower-level and career bureaucrats but also intradepartmental conflict among advocates of the competing interests. Such conflicts may have led, in part, to the breakup of Health, Education, and Welfare into the separate departments of Health and Human Services, and Education. Therefore, secretaries of the newer outer departments will have to contend not only with bureaucratic resistance but also with intradepartmental discord and conflict. These secretaries will be in conflict with their department, and in addition they will have to play the role of broker.

This is not to argue that inner cabinet departments are not plagued by strong interests and intradepartmental conflict. The many desks in the State Department, the intransigence of the Navy Department, and the interservice rivalry in Defense are prime examples. The point here is that management difficulties will be greater in the older outer departments than in the inner ones, and even greater in the newer outer departments. At least this is consistent with Cronin's theory of cabinet department differences.

All of the above, if correct, should lead one to argue that life may be harder and more frustrating for outer cabinet officers than for inner cabinet ones. To make life even bleaker for outer department secretaries, or sweeter for inner cabinet ones, is their comparative relationship to the president. Inner cabinet officials are closer to the president, they act more as presidential advisors, and they are more engaged in policy development, especially big and comprehensive policy (for example, the president's program). Also, it may be none too uncommon to find outer cabinet officials shunted aside, neglected, ignored, or even abused by the president. Thus, though inner cabinet officials may be frustrated in their attempts to run their departments, they may find some job satisfaction in working with the president more closely, more often, and supposedly on more important matters than the outer department secretaries. The outer department secretary's job will be much more heavily oriented toward the frustrating job of departmental management.

If this argument is sound, one should be able to propose some behavioral implications, based on the relative importance of interest groups and closeness of the secretary to the president.

First, let's focus on the impact of job frustration. On the basis of the argument spelled out above, the outer department secretary's job should be more frustrating than that of the inner department secretary (by reasons of departmental resistance, intradepartmental conflict, and distance from the president). If the outer cabinet officer's job is more frustrating, one may hypothesize that they will remain in office for shorter periods than inner cabinet officers. Further, since the newer outer departments are more frustrating than the older ones, their secretaries should leave after even shorter tenures.

Table 47 displays data testing this hypothesis. Data on the average length of tenure of all occupants (including those still in office) provide only mixed support for the hypothesis. While it is true that inner cabinet officers since 1861 stayed in office on the average 37.2 months

TABLE 47

Length of Tenure by Department and Appointment Status, 1861–1984

(in months)

	Initial	All
State	66.5	47.2
Treasury	51.8	45.7
War	29.5	31.2
Justice	42.6	32.3
Navy	41.5	37.4
Defense	87.0	29.6
Postmaster	48.2	41.0
Interior	50.2	43.8
Agriculture	78.0	57.1
Commerce and Labor	36.0	30.0
Commerce	66.0	32.8
Labor	75.4	50.2
HEW	46.3	24.0
HUD	32.9	28.6
Transportation	44.2	27.0
Energy	12.0	28.0
HHS	24.0	20.0
Education	30.0	30.0

Note: For abbreviations, see table 41.

(calculated across departments), which exceeds the average for newer outer cabinet officers (26.3 months), those of the older outer departments have the longest tenure, 42.5 months. Changing the averages to calculations across individuals since 1861 provides the same story (inner secretaries, 38.5 months; older outer secretaries, 43.9 months; newer outer secretaries, 25.9 months).

These findings are consistent with Weisberg (1980), whose data series ended in 1980. There are two problems with the calculations above, though. First, initial and replacement appointees differ in their potential for long service. An initial appointee is constrained only by the length of service of the president, but the replacement is affected also by the length of service of the predecessor. An example can clarify this matter. Two secretaries may serve in the same department during a four-year presidential term, producing an average of 2.0 years. But if the first secretary served for 3.0 years, the replacement could only serve for 1.0 year. A president leaving office so soon after appointment of a replacement to the cabinet may prematurely curtail the replacement's career. For example, it is quite likely that Edmund Muskie would have served longer as secretary of state had Carter been reelected. A cleaner test would separate initial from replacement appointees and focus on the initial ones, whose decisions to stay are less constrained. Similarly, it is probably prudent to exclude from the calculations those still in office. Though their inclusion would have only minor effects on averages for the older departments, they would surely affect the very new departments, the bulk of which are the newer outer departments and are crucial to the hypothesis.

Table 47 removes these two contaminants, and, as expected, in almost all cases the initial appointees served longer than the combination of initial and replacement appointees, a finding that supports the view that replacements do not serve as long as they might be inclined to. Yet, even with these corrections, the same results emerge. Initial secretaries of inner cabinet departments since 1861 served for 48.0 months, older outer secretaries for 60.1 months, and newer outer secretaries for 38.1 months. Averaged across departments the figures are: inner departments, 53.2; older outer departments, 59.0; newer outer departments, 30.6.

One last point needs addressing, and this is the wide variation in service of initial appointees of the three types of department. State Department secretaries serve very long, but War Department secretaries do not. Only for the older outer departments does one find relatively uniform long-term service. This may lead to a modification in the theory presented. It may be that these departments, the most interest group–oriented, are generally headed not by captives but by willing spokespersons for the department's clientele. Such a view is consistent with other studies (Polsby 1978, 1983) and earlier findings presented in chapter 3 concerning recruitment patterns. If these secretaries willingly support the department's single and entrenched interest, then the secretary may encounter little job frustration. Still, there is the potential for conflict with the president, which may produce intense job frustration (for example, Walter Hickel as Nixon's interior secretary). If there is such conflict, it may be exposed by comparing initial and replacement secretaries.

This argument fits into the larger one specified above as well. If a president disagrees with a secretary, it would be only natural for the president to replace that secretary with one who is more likely to support the president. Further, if secretary-president conflict impedes presidential control of the department, the president may seek a replacement who has greater potential for departmental management.

One crude measure of managerial ability of a government agency may be recruitment from the governmental category. Recruitment from the other categories may imply ties to organized interests, and though recruitment from government may not preclude such ties or sympathies, there should also be a strong attitude of government professionalism and service among those who built their careers in the government. Therefore, on the average, this group should be more able to manage a department and also will be less likely to be tied to interests that conflict with presidential policy.

There is some superficial support in the data, presented in table 48. Whereas 37.9 percent of the initial cabinet appointees were recruited from careers primarily in government and politics, 43.8 percent of the replacements were recruited from that sector. The difference, it is true, is modest, but it is in the direction in which other research points (Polsby 1978; Best 1981; King and Riddlesperger 1984).

TABLE 48

Recruitment from Government by Department and Appointment Status, 1861–1984

(in percentages)

	Initial	Replacement
State	50.0	53.8
Treasury	21.1	52.6
War	13.3	50.0
Justice	38.9	30.8
Navy	58.3	23.1
Defense	25.0	14.3
Postmaster	41.2	27.2
Interior	35.0	28.6
Agriculture	26.7	25.0
Commerce and Labor	100.0	33.3
Commerce	0.0	7.1
Labor	11.1	12.5
HEW	75.0	37.5
HUD	0.0	50.0
Transportation	0.0	100.0
Energy	50.0	0.0
HHS	100.0	100.0
Education	50.0	0.0

Note: For abbreviations, see table 41.

When the data are disaggregated by department type, patterns become clear. Inner cabinet replacements since 1861 are somewhat more likely to be recruited from government than initial appointees to those departments, (43.8 percent to 33.7 percent), but the same figures for the newer outer cabinet show very strong tendencies toward recruitment of replacements from government (42.1 percent for replacements, 27.8 percent for initial appointees). However, for the older outer secretaries there is hardly any change (28.8 percent for initial appointees, 23.1 percent for replacements). The outer cabinet departments begin as interest departments, and they seem to stay that way.

One can speculate as to why this might be the case. It may be that the interests entrenched in these departments are not only so firmly in control but are so vital or strong politically that it is hard for any president to withstand their power. Conversely, the comparative weakness of the interests of the two other types of department may give the president a freer hand in appointments, especially of replacements, because the process is less visible and less symbolically important. Further, the relatively small budgets of the older outer cabinet departments and their smaller impacts on the economy may limit presidential interest in attempting to control them. The larger budgets of the other departments, especially the newer outer ones such as Health and Human Services, and the often uncontrollable nature of the programs administered by them may make it a higher priority that the president control them.

Conclusions

In this chapter I have tried to specify more formally components of Cronin's distinction between inner and outer cabinet departments. The broad outline of a theory offered by Cronin was developed, and three hypotheses relating to recruitment patterns, ties to the president, and managerial implications, were stated and tested. All provided some support for the distinction among departments, but with important reservations.

Rather than a simple distinction between inner and outer cabinet departments, a more useful one subdivides the outer cabinet into the older and the newer departments. The basis of this distinction rests on the importance of interests in creating the department and on the complexity of its interest group environment. This tripartite typology suggests a more complex pecking order among departments than the more simple inner-outer distinction offers.

While it is clear that the traditional inner departments are privileged, not all outer departments are severely disadvantaged. Specifically, the older outer departments, those of single interests (Agriculture, Commerce, Labor, and Interior) hold special status such that their interest groups are protected to some degree from presidential desires for control. Rather than the replacement of initial appointees to these departments with "president's men," the selection of replacements continues to be dominated by interest groups. Not even the inner cabinet can boast that kind of insulation.

This interpretation again illustrates the dual nature of the representational system of the cabinet in dealing with political pressures. On the one hand, the inner cabinet squarely places national concerns at the core of the cabinet and the president's attention. However, not all interests are shunted aside. Some, the long-established, entrenched economic interests of the older outer cabinet, are also well represented in the informal hierarchy of cabinet departments.

However, the multiple and competing interests of the multipurpose newer outer departments suffer in this system. Ironically, these departments are often the ones that deal with redistribution issues on a national level, which Lowi (1969) and others suggest are important foci for the president. Yet the more discrete interests of the older outer cabinet seem better served in this cabinet system. However, this does not imply that the interests of the older outer cabinet can push aside the inner cabinet departments and their national concerns.

This dualism between national and special interests reveals again the cabinet's representational role and its attempts to come to grips with these two strong forces, parties and interest groups. The secured position of the older outer cabinet reinforces the picture painted in the earlier chapters of the permeability of the cabinet by the pressures of strong interests. In this sense again one sees the superiority of the cabinet as a representative and political body and its limits as an institutional bureaucracy. The informal hierarchy of cabinet departments is, then, a political and representative solution to a problem. It is not an informal organizational structure aimed at promoting the institutional vigor of the cabinet.

★ 6 ★

A Model

of Cabinet Tenure

The preceding chapters have offered an argument that the cabinet is not well institutionalized. Instead it is a highly political body with strong representative tendencies and qualities. However, the preceeding analysis is limited in a number of respects. The aim of the analysis in this chapter is to attempt to look more directly at the issue of responsiveness, particularly the political and policy responsiveness of individual secretaries. First, consider the limitations of the analysis thus far as it pertains to the question of representation on and by the cabinet.

I have focused on the cabinet's symbolic and policy representativeness. Limitation of the data, however, make it easier to demonstrate symbolic as opposed to policy representation. To show symbolic representation, a weak but sufficient test will discuss the background characteristics of the secretaries and the relationship of those characteristics to important political divisions. This has been done in some detail in chapters 3 and 4. Demonstrating the policy representativeness of the cabinet is more difficult, for it requires data generally unavailable, such as the policy preferences of the secretaries and their actions to promote those or other policies. The background data gathered and used are notoriously poor in answering the question of policy representation, though some inferences based on the combination of data analysis and logic have been offered. This gap on policy representation is important because of the theoretical importance of policy concerns to representation theory.[1]

Further, somewhat missing from the earlier chapter is a sensitive treatment of the responsiveness issue. Representation is not merely a static congruence between representative and represented. It is also an influence relationship, with each party, theoretically, being able to influence the other. The responsiveness issue therefore raises the issue of causality (Eulau and Karps 1978).

I have tried to look at the issue of responsiveness by inspecting the dynamic properties of the cabinet. Thus, by looking at the appearance and disappearance of certain types of secretary, I have tried to make some arguments about the symbolic responsiveness of the cabinet. However, this analysis has noted a major deficiency: its inability to determine the causal agent. Has the cabinet symbolically responded to the public? Has the president symbolically manipulated the cabinet to appeal to the public and build support coalitions? Has a third factor, social transformation, been the causal agent changing both the cabinet and the public? Data only on cabinet change cannot answer the question of causality and responsiveness in any satisfactory manner.

Lastly, the analysis thus far has looked at the cabinet primarily as a collective. Little attention has been accorded the secretaries as individuals. If the arguments of the lack of collective responsibility are correct, then one must begin to look at the cabinet at the individual level. Doing so also has the advantage of reopening the question of policy responsiveness.

Though the recoverable data on cabinet members is silent on their policy preferences in any systematic fashion,[2] data on career patterns may enable us to construct a test of the importance of certain policy conditions to the behaviors of the secretaries. In this chapter I will build a model of cabinet tenure that argues that the decision to stay or leave the cabinet may be viewed in part as a policy decision. As the reader will see shortly, the model is more complex and builds in personal, nonpolicy concerns as well.

Yet these data enable us to raise the question of policy responsiveness on one type of behavior. In a sense, is leaving the cabinet the way that secretaries express an opinion on the policies of the administration? Is this real voting with one's feet or is it more a matter of personal career opportunities lost or to be gained? Though these tenure data do not speak to the full range of responsiveness and policy concerns, this type of behavior is far from trivial.

The Implications of Tenure for the Cabinet

Most research on political careers has focused on recruitment. However, in recent years attention to the problem of reasons why government officials leave office has increased. This is especially true in the case of voluntary retirement from Congress (Hibbing 1982a, 1982b; Cooper and West 1981; Frantzich 1978a, 1978b). Though voluntary retirement has only recently captured the attention of scholars of the Congress, it has long been a concern of scholars of the bureaucracy (Corson and Paul 1966; Bernstein 1958; Stanley, Mann, and Doig 1967; Mann and Doig 1965; Heclo 1977, 1983; Mitnick 1980). In this chapter I ask the question, Why is cabinet tenure so short.

Such a question raises important practical and theoretical concerns. First, it is often mentioned that the "single most obvious characteristic of Washington's political appointees is their transience" (Heclo 1977, 103; see also Kingdon 1984, 32). For instance, from 1789 to 1984, the average cabinet secretary stayed in office for 38 months.

Rapid turnover in these high appointive ranks has important implications. First, some scholars remark that a cabinet member needs a certain amount of time in office in order to understand the department and the job well and to be an effective manager. Further, stability in office helps build working relations among high-level bureaucrats within a department, as well as across departments. A common complaint in Washington is the lack of teamwork among top-level political executives. Short tenure exacerbates this problem (Heclo 1977, 106–09). Also, the resignation of a secretary often leads to an exodus of subcabinet political appointees, who often leave government when their political patron leaves. Thus, personnel instability at the cabinet level may increase that at the subcabinet level (Heclo 1977, 107).

Not only will policy coordination and management suffer because of this instability, but the public image of the administration may also suffer if too rapid turnover is the norm. The public may begin to feel that the president is unable to control his administration or that the administration is rife with conflict. Such an air of instability will surely not serve to comfort the public.

A Cost-Benefit Model of Cabinet Tenure

The guiding assumption underlying the model of cabinet tenure— namely, that secretaries are purposive individuals who rationally pursue their goals—is simple and has been used often. To act rationally, the secretary will weigh costs and benefits and, when costs exceed benefits, will refrain from action or perhaps choose another goal: goals will be pursued only when their benefits outweigh costs.

This assumption is not unreasonable. Much of the literature on building cabinets uses it. For instance, Fenno speaks of a person's availability for office and notes that presidents do not always get their first choice for a particular post—some individuals turn down presidential requests, presumably because the sacrifice is too great or the president's offer is not attractive enough (Fenno 1959, 59–62, 67–77).

Further, there are costs and benefits to staying in the cabinet. For instance, one cost of joining the cabinet, especially for a person in the private sector, would be a reduction in salary. Staying in the cabinet could add to that loss.

However, if the cost of leaving is greater than the cost of staying, an individual will remain in the cabinet, even though doing so may have a negative value. For instance, suppose someone committed to a career in government is recruited from the Congress into the cabinet. One attendant cost would be the sacrifice of a safe seat in Congress. Further, assume that the individual became associated with the promotion of an unpopular policy. Under such a circumstance, the cost of remaining in the cabinet may mount, but the association with the unpopular policy may foreclose any attempts to return to the Congress.[3]

This perspective differs from that of most studies of cabinet building (Fenno 1959; Polsby 1978), which tend to emphasize the president's perspective. Polsby (1978) documents clearly the impact of the president on the composition of the cabinet. However, it is less likely that the president will affect the timing of departure. That is likely only in those rare cases when a president fires a secretary (more on this point later; also, see Weisband and Frank 1975). The secretary's perspective is used here to conceptualize and explain secretarial tenure.

The following sections will build upon and test this model. The cost-benefit calculations will be organized around three types of cost or benefit: characteristics of and relationships to presidents, characteristics of policies, and characteristics of the secretaries. The first two tie directly to our concern with policy responsiveness. The third takes the more standard view of the literature on tenure of executives; that is, that personal considerations determine length of government service.

Characteristics of the President-Secretary Relationship

The characteristics of the presidents under whom a secretary serves may affect the decision to remain or leave. Two factors about the president may be crucial, the degree of conflict between the president and the secretary and the value of the president to the secretary.

President-secretary conflict, whether of a policy or personal nature, may shorten tenure. Conflict may cause the secretary to exit voluntarily or lead the president to fire the secretary. Firings, at least public ones, seem to be rare. If the president wants a secretary removed from office, usually the secretary will comply with little protest (Weisband and Frank 1975, 3–9). Rather than removing secretaries, presidents tend to ignore or isolate them (Cronin 1980, chapter 8). Other than in the inner cabinet, few secretaries are relied upon heavily, and retaining a dissenter, who can be ignored and bypassed through the undersecretaries and bureau heads, may be a more palatable strategy to the president than trying to explain to the public the cause of the conflict with the administration.

However, when conflict arises, the value of the job decreases, and the point may arrive where the cost of the conflict is great enough to lead to the secretary's resignation. I employ three indictors of potential for conflict: party differences between the president and the secretary, loyalty to the president, and type of department headed. Party differences may arouse policy differences and conflict (Aberbach and Rockman 1976). Loyalty may be thought of in both policy and personal terms, and its presence may reduce not only policy, but also personal, conflict.

Developing measures of loyalty from the historical record that are both systematic and cover all secretaries is quite difficult. Consequently, the measures of loyalty are crude, but utilization of a number of different indicators may increase confidence in the results.

Four measures of loyalty are employed: whether the secretary and president come from the same region, whether the secretary exited in the first or second presidential term, whether the secretary campaigned for the appointing president, and whether the president and secretary come from the same state. The first, regional congruence, measures a type of policy loyalty and is justified on the grounds that the parties often possess internal divisions that are regionally based. A secretary from the president's region, then, may be thought of as coming from the presidential wing of the party. Presidents seem to respond to this regional factor, for secretaries from their own region are overrepresented by about 10 percent (see details in chapter 3).

The second, term of exit, measures whether the secretary remains in the cabinet until after the presidential reelection campaign is over. Some secretaries will remain until the new term starts in order to help the president secure another term. Placing presidential reelection goals above their own desire to leave may be a sign of loyalty. There are numerous examples of secretaries remaining until the beginning of the new term, for instance, Terrell Bell, Reagan's education secretary.

Both the region and reelection variables relate to the question of policy responsiveness raised earlier in this chapter. We assume that regional congruence is a surrogate measure for policy congruence, noting its limitations and weaknesses as a measurement. If secretaries from nonpresidential regions leave more swiftly, it may be because of displeasure with policies that the president is pursuing. Similarly, the reelection variable may indicate a policy concern on the part of the secretary, since they delay their exit in order to help the president seek reelection, and perhaps to help continue the president's policies. However, one must also take note of the inherent limitations of these variables and their potential ambiguity on the question of policy responsiveness.

The other two measure a more personal sort of loyalty, perhaps friendship, and thus are more likely to be devoid of policy concerns. That a secretary campaigned for the appointing president may indicate a president repaying a trusted and valued friend. Coming from the same state may indicate longtime friendships. It is often remarked that White House staffs are filled with longtime friends from the president's home state (Florestano 1977). This home state connection may hold for the cabinet as well.

The third indicator of potential conflict is the secretary's department. Discussions of the difference between the inner and outer cabinet usually point to the greater potential and likelihood of conflict between presidents and secretaries of outer cabinet departments. Weisberg (1980) has reported on the differences in tenure of outer and inner secretaries and has demonstrated the usefulness of distinguishing among older and newer outer cabinet departments (see the discussion in chapter 5). The interest group environment of the outer departments, which may pull the secretary away from the administration, and the role of the inner secretary as presidential advisor (Cronin 1980) should hypothetically lead to lower levels of president-secretary conflict in the inner cabinet departments. Of these conflict variables, this may be the one most relevant to policy yet discussed.

Presidents may also be of variable value to the secretaries. For instance, presidential popularity may rub off onto the cabinet secretary, at least in the circles of the politically aware, and such an effect may increase the secretary's political capital. If this is the case, it may be in the secretary's interest to stay in the administration until its natural conclusion. Policy considerations may be important here, for popularity may derive in part from successful administration policies.

To measure presidential popularity, I relied upon the indices of presidential greatness. Though not quite measuring popularity, and though often being distant temporally from the president's administration, these indices measure presidential reputations and crudely group the presidents into those who had reputations for success and those regarded as failures. Such measures are not without their pitfalls: the historical reassessment of presidents such as Truman and Eisenhower may bias their use as measures of presidential reputation during the president's administration, yet it is also true that the reputedly great have tended to stay in that category. Reassessed reputations rarely catapult a president into the great category. Similarly, the abject "failures" tend to stay in that lowly category. To help mute the noise in this measure, I built two dummy variables, one for the great presidents, the other for the "failures." Using a comparison of poll results reported in Cronin (1980, 387–88), I classified eight presidents in the "great" category: Washington, Jefferson, Jackson, Lincoln, Theodore Roosevelt, Wilson, Franklin Roosevelt, and Truman. Less subject to disagreement are the "failures": Monroe, Van Buren, William Harrison, Tyler, Taylor, Fillmore, Pierce, Buchanan, Johnson, Grant, Hayes, Garfield, Arthur, Benjamin Harrison, McKinley, Taft, Harding, Coolidge, Hoover, Nixon, and Ford. Leaving early from administrations classified as failures may be the classic example of the secretary "voting with his feet" about administration policies.

Regression equations of the form below (equation 1) were used to estimate the effects of conflict and presidential reputation on cabinet tenure. The dependent variable is the length of tenure of a cabinet secretary in months. Length of presidential tenure and initial versus replacement appointment are used as controls. The first measures the potential tenure under a particular president. Initial versus replacement appointment also has implications for tenure. Unlike initial appointees, replacements are constrained in how long they might serve. (See the related discussion in chapter 5.) Further, Polsby (1978) argues that initial and replacement secretaries differ because presidents seek generalists with managerial skills to replace the initial appointees, who may have been closely tied to interest groups.

There is one possible problem with this equation and those to follow: multicollinearity. This is especially evident when one considers two variables in equation 1, term of exit (b_{11}) and length of presidential tenure (b_3). By definition, presidents who serve 48 months or less force secretaries to exit in the first term. However, the larger number of secretaries appointed in the second term reduces the correlation between term of exit and length of president's tenure significantly.

Though there is no statistical solution for multicollinearity, its presence may be diagnosed. A recursive F-test was performed on equation 1 in which each variable was dropped from the equation in turn and the F statistic for the full and reduced forms of the equation were compared. This was done for each variable in each model. I also looked at the zero-order relationships of each variable and the intercorrelations of each independent variable for additional information. Though some relationship between the two variables mentioned above was detected, it has no effect on the results reported herein.

Equation 1

Y (cabinet tenure, in months) $=$ a (constant)
$+$ b_1 (regional congruence of president and secretary)
$+$ b_2 (initial appointee)
$+$ b_3 (president's tenure)
$+$ b_4 (older outer cabinet secretary)
$+$ b_5 (inner cabinet secretary)
$+$ b_6 (great president)
$+$ b_7 ("failed" president)
$+$ b_8 (secretary from opposition party)
$+$ b_9 (secretary from president's party)
$+$ b_{10} (secretary who campaigned for appointing president)
$+$ b_{11} (term of exit, 0 $=$ first term, 1 $=$ second)
$+$ b_{12} (state congruence of secretary and president)
$+$ e (error term)

The results of the regression equation are presented in table 49. Various combinations of the variables of equation 1 were run, but only the significant coefficients are shown. Relationship with the president has a small but significant impact on the decision to leave. The control variable, initial appointee status, was quite strong and indicates that initial appointees serve about 14 months longer than their replacements. Term of exit also showed significance, indicating that secretaries extend their tenure into the second presidential term. This variable increases tenure by about 12 months.

This analysis can be refined in two ways. First, a better measure of presidential popularity, which uses yearly averages of the Gallup popu-

TABLE 49
Regression Results of the Impact of Characteristics of the President on Tenure

	1789–1876			1876–1952			1953–1984			All Years		
	b	SE	F	b	SE	F	b	SE	F	b	SE	F
Constant	28.03	3.75	55.95	56.68	9.68	34.22	76.67	8.49	81.54	36.22	13.29	7.45
Initial appointee				19.01	5.80	10.82	24.75	5.10	23.52	14.23	3.69	14.90
Term of exit	15.39	7.54	4.16				12.51	5.91	4.49	12.36	5.23	5.17
Great president	22.13	7.91	7.84									
President's tenure				2.26	.95	5.66						
Failed president							− 11.81	5.84	4.08			
R^2	.10			.08			.33			.07		
Adjusted R^2	.09			.06			.31			.07		
Equation F	7.40			6.89			12.07			10.10		

larity question, can be employed. This entails a large loss of cases since the Gallup questions were aksed only from 1940 on.[4] A bivariate equation employing only the Gallup popularity question shows a mild but significant impact (b = .61, SE = .23, R^2 = .07), but when other variables are added into the equation, the effects of popularity fall out.

A second refinement entails breaking the analysis into periods. One can argue that the character of the cabinet changed over history and that the previous analysis may obscure important relationships that are period specific. Three periods are identified that correspond well to the development of cabinet departments—Washington to Grant (1789–1876), Hayes to Truman (1877–1952), and Eisenhower to Reagan (1953–84). Most of the inner and older outer cabinet departments were created in the first period. The second was one of relative stability in the cabinet: only Commerce and Labor, later separated into two departments, was added. Further, this second period also marks the beginnings of the civil service system. The last period marks the creation of the newer outer cabinet departments, the social service style departments. Other breakdowns can be offered and other cut points suggested, but these roughly correspond to broad and important changes in the cabinet.

Equation 1 was rerun for each of the three periods. Results are displayed in table 49. The most revealing finding is that no variable proved significant for all three periods, though some reached statistical significance for two of the periods. In the first period, appointment status had no impact, as it did on the longer model. However, term of exit reached significance and pointed in the correct direction. The strongest variable was presidential greatness: secretaries who served under great presidents stayed about 22 months longer than those who did not. This finding persists when controlling for the number of years that each president served (great presidents were more likely to serve two terms than "failed" presidents).

In the second period, appointment status reappears as a significant variable. The only other variable to surface in this period is length of tenure of the president. Only our control variables, which affect the opportunity to extend service, had any impact. None of the variables relating to characteristics of the president-secretary relationship proved significant.

The results of the third period are the most striking. Three variables proved important—appointment status, term of exit, and service under a "failed" president. The appointment status variable is strong, much more so than the others, and reveals that initial appointees in this period will serve almost 25 months longer than their replacements. Also, whereas waiting to exit until the second term increases cabinet tenure by 12.5 months, serving under a "failed" president reduces tenure by almost 12 months.

Lastly, the predictive power of the models varies across the periods. The first two show R^2s similar to the whole period and hover in the 8–10 percent range. However, in the third period the R^2 rises to 33 percent, though the bulk is contributed by appointment status. In all, the periodic comparisons proved instructive. Though relationship with the president had some impact in the first and third periods, they showed no effect in the second period.

Characteristics of Policy

The aim of the analysis in this chapter is to detail the impact of policy responsiveness on secretarial tenure. While the presidential relationship model may speak to that issue, most of the variables that were used are at best ambiguously tied to policy concerns. The lack of references to specific policies leads to this ambiguity. In this section, we consider a more policy-specific model.

One may conceptualize policy conditions as environmental factors that affect secretarial decisions to stay or exit. One way to model such factors would be to inspect the policy circumstance of each secretary and each department. Such a procedure would not only be cumbersome and difficult, but it would also lack parsimony and might lead to ad hoc explanations. A different, more satisfying approach would look to policy factors that fall on all the secretaries of the same cabinet simultaneously. The former approach will be dealt with in a fashion in the following sector on individual characteristics, and also has been touched upon with the distinction among departments. The focus here is more on how global policy factors affect tenure decisions.[5]

Two factors readily come to mind. The first is war. If a war is in progress, a barrier to exit may have been erected. A war often entails setting aside partisan and other disputes and rallying together until it is over. Cabinet officers might feel this effect and temporarily set aside personal ambitions for the sake of the nation. In our cost-benefit parlance, wars increase the cost of exiting, though they do not necessarily increase the cost or benefit of the job itself.

On the other hand, major economic dislocations may impel massive cabinet exiting. Administrations blamed for economic downturns do poorly at the polls (the literature on this point is huge), and secretaries may see their political careers threatened by continued association with an administration blamed for a poor economy. Further, economic downturns, panics, recessions, and depressions, may push the secretary's department and program aside or off of the agenda, to be replaced by economic concerns that may frustrate the secretary's policy pursuits. In short, economic conditions may raise the cost of remaining in the cabinet. Equation 2 tests the model.

$$\text{Equation 2}$$

Y (cabinet tenure, in months) = a (constant)
$+\ b_1$ (initial appointee)
$+\ b_2$ (president's tenure)
$+\ b_3$ (war)
$+\ b_4$ (economic downturn)
$+\ e$ (error term)

Again, initial appointment and length of tenure of the appointing president are used as controls. War and economic downturns are operationalized as Copeland did in his study of presidential vetoes (1983, 703–04), with one exception: I do not class the 1804 Tripoli dispute as a major war.

Table 50 presents the regression results for the 1789–1984 series. Both of the control variables, appointment status and president's length of tenure, reached statistical significance, but neither the war nor the economic variable attained that level. However, the wars experienced by the United States were not all of the same stripe—some were popular and others were not. To investigate this hypothesis, I created two variables, one for popular versus unpopular wars, the other a

TABLE 50

Regression Results of the Impact of Characteristics of Policy on Tenure

	1789–1876			1876–1952			1953–1984			All Years		
	b	SE	F	b	SE	F	b	SE	F	b	SE	F
Constant	13.42	12.64	1.12	55.02	10.05	30.03	57.81	11.35	25.91	44.67	6.76	43.69
Initial appointee	2.10	6.57	.10	18.30	5.83	9.86	22.46	5.36	17.55	12.02	3.63	10.96
President's tenure	3.44	1.34	6.55	2.00	.99	4.10	2.44	1.21	4.08	1.89	.70	7.18
Economic downturn	5.78	7.80	.55	1.33	5.88	.05	1.25	8.98	.02	3.98	3.91	1.02
War	−3.34	9.09	.14	12.38	9.32	1.74	4.30	5.61	.59	4.22	5.31	.64
World War II				52.45	16.53	10.04				50.52	16.87	8.94
R^2		.05			.09			.24			.09	
Adjusted R^2		.02			.07			.20			.08	
Equation F		1.83			4.28			5.66			6.53	

dummy variable for each war. Further, the Vietnam War was divided into two segments, one dating through 1967, the other beginning with 1968. This was done to capture the waning popularity of the war after the Tet offensive.

The war popularity variable displayed no significant effects, nor did most of the individual wars. However, World War II exhibited strong impacts and persisted with controls for the economy, other wars, and the control variables. The sign indicates that secretaries serving during this war extended their service, and this is consistent with the line of reasoning offered above. This was perhaps the most popular war in our history, and also the one in which people felt the greatest threat to the nation. Of coincidental importance, Franklin D. Roosevelt also extended his tenure as president because of the impending threat of the war and its occurrence.

The policy model was also disaggregated into the three periods. The results of the longer series are repeated. Neither the economy nor the general war variable had any impact, though the control variables tended to reach significance levels (except for the lack of impact of appointment status in the first period). Also, the World War II variable reached significance in the second period.

Unlike the presidential relationship model, the policy model does not vary by period. However, the results of the World War II variable indicate that, if sensitive policy indicators for each secretary could be created, policy could be an important predictor of secretarial exit. However, the evidence thus far suggests that nonpolicy concerns may be more important in determining cabinet tenure.

Characteristics of the Secretary

One cannot build a career in the cabinet. Though some secretaries may serve in more than one post or under more than one president, the political system makes it wholly unlikely that one may be the secretary of defense until retirement. Therefore, one must be careful to specify the impact of secretarial tenure within the broader outlines of building a career. This leads to the question, Under what circumstances will cabinet service help to foster or inhibit the individual's desired career path?

One may suggest that those recruited from the government category will place a higher value on cabinet service than those recruited from law, education, and business. Those who have already built careers in government may be more committed to service than those from the other categories. They may view cabinet service as the top of a government career, especially when the hurdles to reaching the presidency are so massive.

However, those with primary careers in business may view cabinet service in more idealistic terms and may even sacrifice large salaries and top-level management positions to do their duty. Financial losses may become insupportable and idealism may wear thin over time, and these people may be inclined to leave government service more readily than those recruited from government.

Future job prospects may also affect cabinet service (Schlesinger 1966). For instance, secretaries are often sought by firms in the private sector after their government service is over. Firms may seek secretaries because of their knowledge about government and/or their governmental connections. Thus, outgoing secretaries are often in positions to command lucrative jobs in business. Similarly, law firms and educational institutions and foundations seek ex-secretaries.

On the other hand, the cabinet is about as high as one can fly in the government service. Other than a Senate seat, perhaps a judicial (Supreme Court) appointment, or the presidency or vice presidency, there is no comparable government job to which a secretary can go. Unlike those secretaries bent on returning (or turning) to the private sector, in which case there exist strong incentives to leave government service, the career government officials in the cabinet are at a career dead end. Hence, they have an incentive to remain in the cabinet. Likewise, a secretary bent on retiring has an incentive to stay until the end of the president's term (or until the next election) because there is no great pull out of the cabinet.

Lastly, younger cabinet members may have a greater incentive to stay in order to build a record of accomplishment. Such a record could help further career ambitions, whether they exit into the public or private sector. Older secretaries capping off a career by serving in the cabinet have no great incentive to stay long, though they do not necessarily have an incentive to exit fast, either. Still, their incentive structure should not lead to a cabinet tenure as long as that for younger secretaries. All of these conditions are based on a personal sense of career with little or no policy relevance. These hypotheses are tested with equation 3.

Equation 3

Y (cabinet tenure, in months) $= a$ (constant)

$+ b_1$ (recruitment from government)

$+ b_2$ (recruitment from business)

$+ b_3$ (recruitment from law)

$+ b_4$ (exit into government)

$+ b_5$ (exit into business)

$+ b_6$ (exit into law)

$+ b_7$ (exit into education)

$+ b_8$ (retirement)

$+ b_9$ (age at appointment)

$+ b_{10}$ (appointment status)

$+ b_{11}$ (president's tenure)

$+ e$ (error term)

Appointment status and length of tenure of the appointing president again are used as controls. The recruitment and exit variables are operationalized similarly to Prewitt and McAllister's (1976) concept of career space. The present typology consists of four categories: law, education, business and government. This typology differs slightly from Heclo's (1979, 107–12) four great estates, the private sector, academia, the bureaucracy, and elective government. Primarily, I split the private sector into law and the rest, arguing that the career pattern of lawyers differs substantially from those in the rest of the private sector. Law is specifically operationalized as membership in a law firm (again see the discussion in chapter 3, which details the reasons behind these decisions).[6]

The education category here is broader than Heclo's academia and includes lower-level educational work, educational administration, and foundation employment, as well as university employment. Last, the two types of governmental work were combined, in part because the numbers coming from the bureaucracy are a recent phenomenon and, for most periods, bureaucrats are small in number.

In some cases secretaries held more than one important career. When this occurred, the coders and the principal investigator made a judgment about the most important career style. Usually such judgments were easy to make and were primarily based on the comparative length of the careers and special training for them. The number of these cases was small, however.

Table 51 presents the regression results (only the significant relationships are shown). First, it is impossible to enter the retirement variable into the equation with all of the exit variables simultaneously. Retirement is the inverse of the combination of all postcabinet jobs. Therefore, I initially ran one equation with all four exit variables but without the retirement variable, and then a second equation with only the retirement variable.[7]

The form of the equation made little difference, however, for neither exit nor retirement reached statistical significance. However, exit into the government and retirement almost reached that level. They showed the proper signs, with exit into government shortening careers and retirement lengthening them. One reason for their lack of impact is the effects of age, which reached statistical significance. Age correlates moderately with retirement. The effects of age, which are modest, indicate that younger secretaries stay the longest. Younger secretaries may be using cabinet appointment to help build a political career, and one should note that a few were appointed in their thirties. Lastly, the control variables again reached statistical significance, and the R^2 registered a .09.

Again, the analysis was performed for each of the three periods. Results of these equations are also displayed in table 51 (again, only significant coefficients are shown). In the first period, only age had any impact. The control variables dropped out in its presence. Again, the R^2 ranges as most of the others have: it is .07.

For the other two periods the control variables reappear (only initial appointment status has effects in the middle period), and age again reappears with the negative sign in the second period. The R^2 for the second period again is modest, but for the third period it is quite

TABLE 51

Regression Results of the Impact of Characteristics of the Secretary on Tenure

	1789–1876			1876–1952			1953–1984			All Years		
	b	SE	F	b	SE	F	b	SE	F	b	SE	F
Constant	101.21	20.17	25.20	56.68	9.68	34.33	59.67	10.94	29.81	70.57	14.26	24.50
Initial appointee				19.01	5.80	10.75	22.70	5.29	18.40	13.24	3.67	13.03
Age	−.11	.03	10.49	−.09	.03	5.66				−.04	.02	4.01
President's tenure							2.50	1.18	4.45	2.62	.67	15.21
R^2	.07			.08			.24			.08		
Adjusted R^2	.07			.06			.21			.07		
Equation F	7.25			6.89			11.23			8.13		

healthy at .24, though only the control variables are contributing. In all, secretarial characteristics have only modest impact throughout, as only age showed impact. Recruitment and exit patterns did not significantly affect length of tenure.

Combined Impacts

Lastly, consider the joint effects of the three models. Significant variables from the three equations were pooled and run in one final equation. Results are presented in table 52.

First, one control variable, the length of tenure of the president, did not reach significance, though its companion, appointment status, did. Initial appointees serve over 13 months longer than their replacements. Second, the World War II variable remained in the equation and exhibited a pronounced positive impact on cabinet tenure. The only other variable with significant impact was term of exit. The other variables previously found significant, presidential greatness or "failure" and age, did not remain significant in this fuller equation. Lastly, the R^2, at .11, did not improve much over previous trials.

Different combinations of variables were found important across the different periods, however, implying a historically changing exit calculus. In the first period neither of the control variables was important, but both age and presidential greatness were. Again, younger secretaries stayed longer, almost one month for each year by which they were younger than the other secretaries. Over a forty-year age spread,[8] this can add to 3 or more years of extra service. Presidential greatness also had pronounced effects and added about 22 months of service. One must remember, also, that though great presidents are more likely to serve longer than "failed" ones, this greatness effect persists in the face of controls for the length of tenure of the president and the term of exit of the secretary. Lastly, as in the equation with the longer time frame, the R^2 for this one was modest at best at .12.

During the second period, one control variable, appointment status, returns in importance, but the World War II variable overshadows the impact of the control. No other variable reaches significance. In all,

TABLE 52

Regression Results of the Impact of Characteristics of President, Policy, and Secretary on Tenure

	1789–1876			1876–1952			1953–1984			All Years		
	b	SE	F	b	SE	F	b	SE	F	b	SE	F
Constant	88.73	20.14	19.45	64.84	8.70	55.65	76.67	8.49	81.54	73.22	13.50	29.38
Initial appointee				16.98	5.52	9.49	24.75	5.10	23.52	13.62	3.68	13.69
World War II				65.13	16.42	15.76				53.09	15.81	11.29
Term of exit										14.82	4.13	12.89
Age	−.96	.32	8.47									
Great president	22.05	7.73	8.18									
Failed president							−11.81	5.84	4.08			
R²	.10			.08			.33			.11		
Adjusted R²	.11			.12			.31			.10		
Equation F	9.71			12.17			12.07			9.77		

appointment status increases tenure during this period by almost 17 months, while the war's effect amounted to some 65 months. Part of the reason for this great effect was that many of Roosevelt's wartime secretaries also served in his earlier administrations. Yet the war effect is significant in itself because those other effects, the number of years that Roosevelt served, were statistically controlled and did not substantially alter the effect of the war variable. Again, the R^2 was similar in magnitude to the others noticed, reaching .13.

Lastly, the final period shows not only the most complex structure, but also the greatest predictive power. First, appointment status continued its significance. Term of exit and "failed" presidents also added to the equation's power. Though not as strong as the appointment variable, term of exit increased tenure by over 12 months, while serving under a presidential "failure" decreased tenure by almost 12 months, thereby almost wiping out the effects of loyalty to the president. Most significantly, the equation's R^2 towers over the others, hitting .33. While it is true that the control variable accounts for the bulk of the explained variance, the addition of the other two variables increases the R^2 by almost 10 percent. Lastly, the periodic breakdown shows a different exit pattern for each period.

Conclusions and Implications

The aim of the analysis presented in this chapter was to determine if policy concerns affect the tenure decisions of cabinet officers and to relate the findings to questions of the individual policy responsiveness of secretaries. Results on the whole were disappointing. Though it is true that some policy variables, notably the World War II variable, demonstrated pronounced impact, most failed to reach statistical significance. Further, the set of variables classified as characteristics of the president-secretary relationship, which had the potential for including policy concerns, also fell short of the mark.

What does this say about the policy responsiveness of the secretaries? First, such responsiveness is probably limited, though, as the war and presidential greatness/failure variables indicate, under proper conditions, policy may have an impact. However, before being too glum, I must remind the reader that only one decision was studied, that it was studied indirectly, and that other, more policy-relevant decisions exist. Therefore, though the book is open on the potential for policy responsiveness, all that we can say is that policies have limited effect on the decision to leave.

Conclusion

Almost thirty years ago, Fenno wrote about the institutional development of the cabinet during the Eisenhower administration. From the late 1930s through the Eisenhower years, rapid institutionalization in the executive branch was the norm. However, the cabinet's institutional enhancement under Eisenhower was not a part of that larger movement. As soon as Kennedy assumed office, much of Eisenhower's institutional development of the cabinet was dismantled. Whatever Eisenhower changed about the cabinet and Kennedy reversed was due to their personal preferences about the type of cabinet that they wanted, not to its internal characteristics.

The cabinet, in our presidential system, cannot fully claim to be an institution. It has no collective responsibility beyond service and loyalty to a president. It cannot make binding collective decisions on its members. It has no ultimate political responsibility: responsibility rests with the president who appoints the secretaries.

The cabinet is a rather anemic political organization, one without much power or responsibility. Yet cabinet posts are often filled with ambitious and powerful politicians. Why? Primarily because individuals in the cabinet may personally accrue much power. Some of this may be due to the department that they head. State, defense, and treasury secretaries often are able to have a decided effect on policy within their department's domain. However, these individual career benefits do not explain why the cabinet has persisted for so long or why presidents often seek the powerful and ambitious, some who may be rivals to the president, for the cabinet.

The cabinet serves another important purpose for the president and the executive branch. It is able to represent political interests and demands, and through its representative qualities, it supplies the president with a way of repaying and/or attracting supporters.

The Cabinet and Representation Theory

Representation is a complex relationship with many faces and dynamics. Most discussions of representation are limited to either legislators or other elected officials. The legislative and elective focus of representation theory has identified four forms of representative relationships; policy responsiveness, symbolic responsiveness, service responsiveness, and allocative responsiveness (Eulau and Karps 1978). For the cabinet case, only the first two, the symbolic and the policy, are relevant.

That secretaries are not elected limits their ability and motivation to be held accountable. Therefore, to speak of the secretary as representative refers to a limited form of representation. Yet, the circumscribed representative role of the secretary does not also imply that the role is unimportant or without political consequences. Throughout this study I have tried to show how this representative role comes into play and its political importance, especially in reference to interest groups, the parties, and the differences among the several departments. In the remainder of this section, I review and assess the symbolic and policy responsiveness of the cabinet.

The Cabinet and Policy Responsiveness

The major difficulty in assessing definitively the policy responsiveness of the cabinet relates to our inability to assess directly the causal relationship between the secretaries and their constituents. This derives in part from our inability to identify an unambiguous secretarial constituency, as well as our inability to study secretarial decisions. For both, constituency and decision, I had to infer. Inferences, though they may be good educated guesses, are not hard data, nor are they indisputable. Hence, most assessments remain speculative, and though I prefer to approach this assessment conservatively, it may be theoretically useful to throw caution to the winds at times. I hope the reader will take these leaps from the data with a grain of salt and a sense of adventure.

One way to assess, albeit crudely, the policy responsiveness of secretaries is to look at their social background. This raises the question of interest representation, which is at the core of cabinet politics. Interest representation relates to a number of interconnected issues. Presidents appoint cabinet members who can attract or help retain voters. In this sense they are representing some interest in the president's administration, the coalition of presidential support groups in the cabinet. The electoral motivation on the part of the president may subsequently undermine policy harmony in the cabinet, however.

Not all of the background characteristics relate in any clean fashion to policy responsiveness, though. Of the four used, education, age, region, and occupation, perhaps only the latter two are useful.

Both regional and occupational compositional dynamics indicate potential policy responsiveness in the cabinet. Regional policy differences are often quite strong in U.S. politics. First, presidents tend to choose secretaries from their own region. While this may be caused by more than just the president's desire to build a cabinet whose members hold the same policy preferences as the president, regional similarity between the president and the secretaries may enhance policy congruence between the two.

Occupational makeup may also have implications for policy responsiveness. The main finding here is that, when combining length of tenure considerations with occupational background, we were able to build a case that the cabinet changed from one where private sector recruits were motivated to serve because of a sense of duty during the first 30 years of this century, to one where service was motivated more from big government, interest group liberalism, and politico-economic benefit. During this most recent period, considerations of private gain, either personal or business related, may have taken on more importance than duty and obligation. At least this trend is consistent with other interpretations of U.S. government and policy during this century.

Though the cabinet seems to have some ability to represent interests, either regional or economic, it also is a site for the representation of partisan concerns. Secretaries are likely to be members of the president's party. Further, their attachment to the parties has strengthened and weakened with the tides of party organizational strength in the nation. Hence, we may infer some level of fidelity to party in the cabinet, though other data, that on replacements and length of tenure, limit how strongly we can speak of the cabinet as a party apparatus. Party government is not the norm in the United States, nor is it the norm for the cabinet. However, party concerns are not irrelevant to the cabinet either.

The theory of cabinet department differences, the distinction between inner and outer cabinet departments, also leads us to infer the potential for policy responsiveness. The distinction between inner and outer departments not only presents us with an informal status hierarchy among the departments but also suggests that national policy concerns will prevail in most competitions with local and special interest policy preferences at the cabinet level. Generally, the distinctions between departments held up when implications of the theory were tested, though the theory needed refinement. That is, outer cabinet departments were found to be of two subtypes, the older departments and the newer ones. Older outer departments held more secure policy positions than the newer ones. However, the inner departments seemed to hold even more secure positions. The informal organization of cabinet departments may have important policy implications, especially when national interests are distinguished from special and local interests.

Lastly, I looked at the decision to exit from the cabinet, which may indicate another dimension of possible policy responsiveness. At this level, policy considerations were overwhelmed by personal concerns, and the little support for policy impacts that was detected was not unambiguously supportive. Leaving may be a vote of no confidence by the secretary for the president's policies, but personal reasons seem more important.

In all, the cabinet has some potential to be called policy responsive.

It is not the most policy-responsive of bodies, but we should not have expected it to be so. Secretaries are not elected. Hence a strong motivation toward policy responsiveness is missing.

The Cabinet and Symbolic Responsiveness

The lack of collective cabinet accountability and responsibility limits its potential policy responsiveness. Without their being elected, without their bearing responsibility for their policy decisions, incentives for secretaries to be policy responsive are somewhat diminished. However, on the symbolic level we may find the true strength of the cabinet as a representative body.

President's parade their newly formed cabinets before the public in hopes of symbolizing the colors, tone, and coalition make-up of the administration. In the early days of each new administration, the media are filled with information about the president and his administration. And as time progresses and secretaries leave and are replaced, the lens of media attention again focuses on the cabinet's membership.

While this public attention is often focused on the policy ramifications of cabinet membership, attention is also given to the symbolic. The importance of the symbolic derives in part from the political uses of symbolism and the way it relates the administration to the public. Among the political uses are presidential messages of repayment to supportive voters in the past election and perhaps lures to other voters who may be swayed into the president's camp. Thus, coalition maintainance and enhancement are important political goals to be reached by symbolically manipulating the cabinet.

At the same time, symbolic manipulation may make people feel either included in or excluded from the presidential governing coalition. Symbols may be used to make people feel a part of or not a part of political systems. Presidents with wide and deep support probably are more able than those with thin, shallow, and fragile support coalitions to build cabinets that are symbolically diverse.

The characteristics of the secretaries may be important political symbols open to presidential manipulation. To most individuals, the secretaries comprise a nameless crowd. But many may be aware of the types of people filling key cabinet spots, their wealth, regional origin, ethnic group membership, and the like. Hence, the data on backgrounds of secretaries may be of some special utility in understanding the symbolic dimensions of cabinet politics.

Three of the background characteristics, age, region, and occupation, waxed and waned across time, implying some symbolic responsiveness. Though the causal agent may be hard to identify with any certitude, we can offer some reasonable guesses.

First, the aging of the cabinet in the early years probably signaled a stabilizing of the newly formed government. The hectic days of revolution had ceased, and a new era of governing and nation building was setting in. However, the aging process seemed to peak in the early decades of the nineteenth century at about forty to fifty years of age, indicating a rotation of political leadership that is consonant with democratic processes and ideology. That the cabinet did not ossify and become transformed into a gerontological leadership, as other revolutionary movements had (for example, in Russia and China), was an important symbol to the nation of the vitality and functioning of the democratic electoral practices that the revolutionary leaders promised. Electoral processes, therefore, probably were key in explaining the middle-aging of the cabinet.

Similarly, regional shifts in cabinet composition may be tied to electoral shifts. For a century after the Civil War, the South was almost totally frozen out of Republican cabinets. This was symbolically important because of the regional division that the war exacerbated and the party allegiances that formed around these regional animosities. Waving the bloody shirt of the Civil War was an important rallying gesture and campaign theme for Republicans until about the 1960s. That southerners may now find their way onto Republican cabinets may indicate a nationalization of the party system that has healed these regional wounds. In other words, southern membership of Republican cabinets may symbolize the reintegration of the South into national politics.

Regional composition is also a function of population, and as the West has grown in population, its representation on the cabinet has increased. This again symbolizes the importance for the president of coalition maintenance and enhancement, and it again demonstrates the importance of elections in promoting symbolic responsiveness on the part of cabinet.

Occupational transformations, while they may indicate a responsiveness that is electorally motivated, may actually be more acutely affected by larger social transformations and requirements imposed on the job of cabinet member. In the early years, political skills were most important; hence representation of politicians was high. But as government grew, different types of talents and experience, for example in business or the bureaucracy, were required or thought important. Further, as society became more complex because of modernization currents, the generalist (lawyer) was replaced by the specialist (educator, bureaucrat, businessman). This transformation is more in line with Lasswell's skills transformation theory than with the electoral theory presented above and suggests that the cabinet may symbolically relate to secular as well as electoral transformations.

However, the last background characteristic inspected, education, reveals little responsive potential, but this may be highly symbolically important. The cabinet began as an educated elite and remained that way despite the educational improvement of the public over time. What is important here is that education sets the cabinet off from the general populace and secures its place as an elite. While elites in other nations may be defined by lineage, the new democracy had to remove the hereditary factor. Similarly, democratic pressures limited the ability of an oligarchy of wealth to take hold.

However, though educational attainment in the early years may be a mark of family wealth, it need not always be so. Rather, the symbolic importance of education to the running of the early government may be in its signal that the brightest would rule in service to the many. Here education may be equated with intelligence by the public (however disputable the point may be). The symbolic importance of identifying the governing elite in this way lay in the ability to build confidence about the new government. "Those who know about things" would be directing the nation's course. In the competition with possibly hostile nations, though the new nation might not be strong militarily or economically, it could be led by shrewd men. And as the nation grew in power and the world became more complex, the need for men and women of education in the highest councils of government did not diminish. Thus, the stability of the educational attainment of secretaries is symbolically important, if not democratically responsive.

Lastly, the partisan coloration of cabinets has symbolic impact. The more heavily partisan, the more public partisans may be attracted or repelled by the president's cabinet. Recall for instance the unprecedented low levels of public support for Ronald Reagan among Democrats in the early days of his administration, an administration that proved to be among the most partisan in recent memory.

Further, the partisan composition of the cabinet and the strength of partisan attachment of the secretaries may inform the public about the possible influence of special interests. Where partisan attachment is widespread and deep, the cabinet may appear less prone to the influence of special interests. And in this sense the president may be able to argue more convincingly that he is the nation's leader, not just a servant of special interests.

At the same time, and ironically, the more partisan the cabinet is, the more members of interests closely aligned with the major parties may feel attracted or repelled by the administration. And many interests have decided to align themselves with one or the other party, rather than playing the role of nonpartisan advocate.

To summarize, the cabinet's symbolic importance lies in the message that it can send to the nation. That message details who the administration likes, who the administration wants to serve and help, and hence, whether a voter feels a part of the national administration. Such messages of inclusion or exclusion are important, and the make-up of the cabinet informs the public about presidential intentions.

The Democratic Division of Labor

Modern mass democracies are pulled in two, often conflicting, directions. On the one hand, these democracies were created to act on public demands. They were envisioned as having the governmental capacity to meet the public demands placed on them. The ability to act is not unique to democratic government: it is a common requirement of all forms of government.

However, what distinguishes democracy from the other forms of government is the requirement that it represent. At its most basic level, representation requires that government be accessible to the opinions of the represented, that the government at a minimum, listen. Without such an openness, action consonant with public desires and preferences would be diminished greatly.

Listening often inhibits the ability to act. Listening means lowering boundaries with the environment and lessening internal autonomy, and in general it diminishes the capacity to act forcefully and swiftly. Sometimes openness may proceed to the point where inaction results, as some critics suggested occurred as a result of the reforms of Congress in the mid-1970s.

Historically, most governments have decided that the capacity to act was more important than the need to represent. Hence, history is more about the numerous monarchies, aristocracies, oligarchies, and dictatorships, than about democratic governments. Part of the fragility of democratic government may stem from these often conflicting pressures. One solution to the problem of meeting both the demands of representation and the need to act may be to separate the two and to place them in different parts of the government.

We may view our form of government, with its separation of powers, as one solution, in which the legislative branch has been given primary representative responsibility and the executive has been given the capacity to act. It is true that within each branch one finds some elements of both tasks. For instance, Congress has traditionally allowed the money committees special rules protections from amendments and open debate, which allow some congressional action. Similarly, the president, who sits atop the executive, feels democratic pressures through the election process. However, the two branches seem tilted toward their "natural" roles.

The lack of institutional capacity in the cabinet and its greater representative abilities can be thus understood. It is ironic that a body in the executive branch could be so much more representative than capable of acting. But, when viewing the cabinet as but one part of the greater executive branch, one may see that its representative qualities help balance the command and control biases of the bureaucracy. However, by being a voice of representation in an otherwise action-oriented branch, the power of the cabinet is limited, its secretaries and the body as a whole may become alienated from the bureaucracy, and conflict may ensue. We can see the heightening of alienation with the creation of the Executive Office of the President, which was intended to give the president greater control over the bureaucracy. Not too curiously, the more political and representative cabinet was shunted aside. Its role is somewhat at odds with much of the executive branch.

All of this may result in an institutionally weak cabinet, but the greater payoff may be in strengthening the larger government by allowing it to be both capable of acting and able to represent. Though these two tasks may occur mostly at different places, they may both be occurring at the same time. Hence, we may understand the political importance of the cabinet as well as its institutional weakness.

Appendix

Notes

Bibliography

Index

Appendix

Primary Occupation by Department, 1789–1984

(in percentages)

	Law	Government	Business	Education	N
State	26.8	63.4	7.3	2.4	41
Treasury	18.5	46.3	35.1	0.0	54
War	31.3	50.9	17.6	0.0	51
Justice	52.2	44.8	0.0	3.0	67
Navy	23.9	45.6	30.4	0.0	46
Defense	18.2	18.2	54.5	9.1	11
Postmaster	24.6	43.8	24.6	7.0	57
Interior	39.5	34.2	23.7	2.6	38
Agriculture	17.4	26.1	39.1	17.4	23
Commerce and Labor	25.0	50.0	25.0	0.0	4
Commerce	4.5	4.5	81.8	9.0	22
Labor	11.8	11.8	52.9	23.6	17
HEW	8.3	50.0	16.7	25.0	12
HUD	50.0	25.0	12.5	12.5	8
Transportation	37.5	25.0	37.5	0.0	8
Energy	0.0	0.0	100.0	0.0	3
HHS	0.0	100.0	0.0	0.0	2
Education	0.0	50.0	0.0	50.0	2

Note: HEW: Health, Education, and Welfare;
HUD: Housing and Urban Development;
HHS: Health and Human Services.

181

APPENDIX TABLE 2
Previous Political Experience, 1789–1984
(in percentages)

	Party Office	Candidacy	Office	State Campaign	Presidential Campaign	Fund-Raising	Appointment
State	17.1	68.3	85.4	0.0	4.9	0.0	2.4
Treasury	30.9	61.8	78.2	7.3	5.5	0.0	9.1
War	21.2	71.2	82.7	0.0	5.8	1.9	3.8
Justice	25.4	59.7	83.6	6.0	11.9	1.5	8.9
Navy	19.6	73.9	76.1	2.2	8.7	0.0	8.7
Defense	18.2	27.3	54.5	0.0	9.1	0.0	0.0
Postmaster	43.9	37.9	73.7	8.8	14.0	7.0	12.3
Interior	47.4	73.7	89.5	2.6	13.2	5.3	7.9
Agriculture	17.4	52.2	60.9	4.3	0.0	0.0	0.0
Commerce and Labor	25.0	0.0	100.0	0.0	0.0	0.0	0.0
Commerce	27.3	13.6	45.5	4.6	0.0	9.1	0.0
Labor	5.9	11.8	29.4	0.0	5.9	0.0	0.0
HEW	25.4	41.7	75.0	16.7	16.7	16.7	8.3
HUD	12.5	12.5	37.5	12.5	0.0	0.0	0.0
Transportation	25.0	50.0	62.5	12.5	25.0	12.5	12.5
Energy	0.0	33.3	66.7	66.7	0.0	0.0	0.0
HHS	100.0	50.0	100.0	50.0	0.0	0.0	0.0
Education	100.0	0.0	50.0	50.0	0.0	0.0	0.0

Note: Party Office—held a state or local party office;
Candidacy—was a candidate for elective office;
Office—held an elective or appointive office;
State Campaign—worked in a state or local election campaign;
Fund-Raising—helped in fund-raising;
Presidential Campaign—worked in a presidential election campaign;
Appointment—was appointed by the president for whom he or she campaigned.
For abbreviations, see appendix table 1.

APPENDIX TABLE 3
Region of Origin by Department, 1789–1984
(in percentages)

	East	South	Midwest	West
State	59.5	24.3	16.2	0.0
Treasury	52.8	13.2	34.0	0.0
War	50.0	25.0	22.9	2.1
Justice	58.2	16.4	19.4	6.0
Navy	56.8	29.5	11.4	2.1
Defense	50.0	0.0	40.0	10.0
Postmaster	42.1	15.0	40.4	1.8
Interior	8.1	10.8	51.4	29.7
Agriculture	26.1	0.0	56.5	17.4
Commerce and Labor	50.0	0.0	25.0	25.0
Commerce	54.5	18.2	22.7	4.5
Labor	53.8	15.4	15.4	15.4
HEW	40.0	20.0	20.0	20.0
HUD	42.9	14.3	28.6	14.3
Transportation	42.9	14.3	0.0	42.9
Energy	0.0	66.7	0.0	33.3
HHS	100.0	0.0	0.0	0.0
Education	0.0	50.0	0.0	50.0

Note: For abbreviations, see appendix table 1.

Congruence of Political Party by Department, 1789–1984
(in percentages)

	Secretary's Party		
	Same as President's	Different from President's	Unknown
State	65.9	24.4	9.8
Treasury	76.4	16.4	7.3
War	69.2	17.3	13.5
Justice	67.2	22.4	10.4
Navy	76.1	21.7	2.2
Defense	90.9	0.0	9.1
Postmaster	80.7	10.5	8.8
Interior	84.2	10.5	5.3
Agriculture	69.6	4.3	26.1
Commerce and Labor	75.0	25.0	0.0
Commerce	72.7	13.6	13.6
Labor	52.9	5.9	23.5
HEW	91.7	0.0	8.3
HUD	87.5	0.0	12.5
Transportation	75.0	0.0	25.0
Energy	100.0	0.0	0.0
HHS	100.0	0.0	0.0
Education	0.0	0.0	100.0

Note: For abbreviations, see appendix table 1.

APPENDIX TABLE 5

Organizational Actives in President's Party by Department, 1789–1984

(in percentages)

State	22.2
Treasury	45.2
War	25.0
Justice	44.4
Navy	25.7
Defense	30.0
Postmaster	52.2
Interior	50.0
Agriculture	25.0
Commerce and Labor	33.3
Commerce	37.5
Labor	16.7
HEW	36.4
HUD	14.3
Transportation	66.7
Energy	66.7
HHS	100.0
Education	0.0

Note: An organizational active did at least one of the following: held a position in a state or local party organization; worked in a state or local campaign; worked in a presidential campaign; was a fund-raiser. For abbreviations, see appendix table 1.

APPENDIX TABLE 6
Congruence of Secretary's and President's Home State,
1789–1984
(in percentages)

State	13.9
Treasury	18.2
War	11.5
Justice	13.4
Navy	13.0
Defense	0.0
Postmaster	15.8
Interior	10.5
Agriculture	4.3
Commerce and Labor	50.0
Commerce	13.6
Labor	5.9
HEW	16.7
HUD	0.0
Transportation	12.5
Energy	0.0
HHS	0.0
Education	0.0

Note: For abbreviations, see appendix table 1.

APPENDIX TABLE 7
Length of Tenure by Department and Appointment Status, 1789–1984
(in months)

	Initial	All
State	60.7	38.3
Treasury	47.5	36.6
War	35.4	33.2
Justice	39.7	33.0
Navy	37.3	35.0
Defense	87.0	29.6
Postmaster	43.9	36.8
Interior	49.9	36.8
Agriculture	78.0	57.1
Commerce and Labor	36.0	30.0
Commerce	66.0	32.8
Labor	75.4	50.2
HEW	46.3	24.0
HUD	32.9	28.6
Transportation	44.2	27.0
Energy	12.0	28.0
HHS	24.0	20.0
Education	30.0	30.0

Note: For abbreviations, see appendix table 1.

APPENDIX TABLE 8

Recruitment from Government by Department and Appointment Status, 1789–1984

(in percentages)

	Initial	Replacement
State	68.2	57.9
Treasury	30.8	58.6
War	37.0	64.0
Justice	45.8	44.2
Navy	47.4	44.4
Defense	25.0	14.3
Postmaster	45.8	42.4
Interior	31.8	37.5
Agriculture	26.7	25.0
Commerce and Labor	100.0	33.3
Commerce	0.0	7.1
Labor	11.1	12.5
HEW	75.0	37.5
HUD	0.0	50.0
Transportation	0.0	100.0
Energy	50.0	0.0
HHS	100.0	100.0
Education	50.0	0.0

Note: For abbreviated names of departments, see Appendix Table 1.

Notes

Chapter 1. The Cabinet in the U.S. Political System

1. Mackenzie does not note that Cushing did serve as Franklin Pierce's attorney general from 1853 through 1857. See Sobel 1977.

2. Strauss served as commerce secretary on an interim basis but was removed when it was apparent that confirmation would not be forthcoming.

3. Article II, Section 4 reads, "The President, Vice-President, and all civil Officers of the United States shall be removed from Office on Impeachment for, and Conviction of, Treason, Bribery, or other high Crimes and Misdemeanors."

Chapter 2. The Institutionalization of the Cabinet

1. But note the role of Congress as discussed in chapter 1.

2. However, if the secretary does win, the dispute may not be publicly aired. Hence, we have no way of knowing how common this is, but it is probably rare.

3. Hess (1976) stresses this role, which is often ignored by critics of the cabinet.

4. Laski (1940) notes that cabinet service was often viewed as an interruption of another career path. Compare this with Polsby's (1968) discussion of the Congress.

5. For a somewhat different argument see Greenstein 1982 and Duram 1978.

6. However, see Heclo's (1983) assessment.

7. Reagan seems to have successfully countered this tendency. See Nathan 1983.

Chapter 3. The Social Bases of the Cabinet

1. There is a small literature on representative bureaucracy. See Krislov and Rosenbloom 1981; Meier and Nigro 1976; and Subramanian 1969.

2. Data on birth dates were missing mostly in the early years of the Republic because either that information was unrecorded or cabinet members came from foreign countries that also did not keep birth records.

3. Perhaps some for whom age is unknown in the first era were also older. Thus era 1's true mean age might increase and it might not differ much from the other eras.

4. Figure 1 shows where secretaries from the various primary occupation categories end up after leaving the cabinet. Table 23 reverses the perspective and asks where the secretaries in each exit category came from.

Chapter 4. Party Politics and the Cabinet

1. There are only 2 Democratic-Republican organizational actives of 21 total Democratic-Republicans here.

2. However, this strategy is irrelevant if the president does not initially appoint any opposition party members.

3. Also recall John Ehrlichman's famous quip that cabinet secretaries "go off and marry the natives" (cited in Nathan 1975, 40).

Chapter 5. The Secretaries and the Departments

1. The 1789-1984 figures are 27.8 percent and 52.2 percent.

2. Here I have excluded the Labor Department from calculations. Labor may be one department where Republicans are forced to look outside their party. With Labor included, as expected, the figure drops to 78.4 percent.

3. The older outer cabinet figure excludes the Post Office because of the special political patronage nature of that department. With Post Office included, the figure becomes 9.4 percent.

Chapter 6. A Model of Cabinet Tenure

1. For instance, Edelman's (1964) theory of symbolic politics can be seen as the difference between symbolic and policy representativeness.

2. Biographies and autobiographies may provide a nonsystematic source of such information.

3. This framework is quite similar to Hibbing 1982b.

4. The years for which the question is reported are 1940 and 1946–84.

5. It probably is true that secretaries react to different policies differently. Thus, the statistical power of this model will be limited, but it is theoretically important to know if policies that fall across secretaries affect their decisions systematically.

6. Many secretaries were trained in law but did not practice.

7. Secretaries who died in office were excluded from the analysis.

8. Age on appointment ranges from the thirties to the seventies.

References

Aberbach, Joel D., and Bert A. Rockman. 1976. "Clashing Beliefs Within the Executive Branch: The Nixon Administrative Bureaucracy." *American Political Science Review* 70:456–68.

Beck, Paul Allen. 1979. "The Electoral Cycle and Patterns of American Politics." *British Journal of Political Science* 9:129–56.

Bernstein, Marver H. 1958. *The Job of the Federal Executive.* Washington, D.C.: Brookings Institution.

Best, James J. 1981. "Presidential Cabinet Appointments: 1953–1976." *Presidential Studies Quarterly* 11:62–66.

Burnham, Walter Dean. 1970. *Critical Elections and the Mainsprings of American Politics.* New York: Norton.

Chambers, William N., and Walter Dean Burnham, eds. 1975. *The American Party Systems.* 2nd ed. New York: Oxford University Press.

Clubb, Jerome M., William H. Flanigan, and Nancy H. Zingale. 1980. *Partisan Realignment: Voters, Parties, and Government in American History.* Beverly Hills, Calif.: Sage.

Cole, Richard L., and David A. Caputo. 1979. "Presidential Control of the Senior Civil Service: Assessing the Strategies of the Nixon Years." *American Political Science Review* 73:388–413.

Congressional Quarterly, 1976. *Powers of Congress.* Washington, D.C.: Congressional Quarterly Press.

Cooper, Joseph, and William West. 1981. "The Congressional Career in the 1970's." In L. Dodd and B. Oppenheimer, eds., *Congress Reconsidered,* 2d ed. Washington, D.C.: Congressional Quarterly, Inc., pp. 83–106.

Copeland, Gary W. 1983. "When Congress and the President Collide: Why Presidents Veto Legislation." *Journal of Politics* 45:696–710.

Corson, John J., and R. Shale Paul. 1966. *Men Near the Top: Filling Key Posts in the Federal Service.* Baltimore, Md.: Johns Hopkins Press.

Cronin, Thomas E. 1980. *The State of the Presidency.* 2d ed. Boston: Little, Brown.

Dodd, Lawrence C., and Richard L. Schott. 1979. *Congress and the Administrative State.* New York: John Wiley.

Duram, James C. 1978. " 'A Good Growl': The Eisenhower Cabinet's January 16, 1959 Discussion of Federal Aid to Education." *Presidential Studies Quarterly* 8:434–43.

Edelman, Murray. 1964. *The Symbolic Uses of Politics.* Urbana: University of Illinois Press.

Eulau, Heinz, and Paul D. Karps. 1978. "The Puzzle of Representation: Specifying Components of Responsiveness." In H. Eulau and J. Wahlke, eds., *The Politics of Representation: Continuities in Theory and Research.* Beverly Hills, Calif.: Sage, pp. 55–71.

Fenno, Richard R., Jr. 1959. *The President's Cabinet.* Cambridge, Mass.: Harvard University Press.

———. 1978. *Home Style: House Members in Their Districts.* Boston: Little, Brown.

Fishel, Jeff. 1973. *Party and Opposition.* New York: McKay.

Fisher, Louis. 1978. *The Constitution Between Friends: Congress, the President, and the Law.* New York: St. Martin's.

Florestano, Patricia S. 1977. "The Characteristics of White House Staff Appointees from Truman to Nixon." *Presidential Studies Quarterly* 7:184–91.

Frantzich, Stephen E. 1978a. "De-Recruitment: The Other Side of the Congressional Equation." *Western Political Quarterly* 31:105–26.

———. 1978b. "Opting Out: Retirement from the House of Representatives." *American Politics Quarterly* 6:251–73.

Funston, Richard. 1975. "The Supreme Court and Critical Elections." *American Political Science Review* 69:795–811.

Gibson, James L., Cornelius P. Cotter, John F. Bibby, and Robert J. Huckshorn. 1983. "Assessing Party Organizational Strength." *American Journal of Political Science* 27:194–222.

Gilmour, Robert S. 1975. "The Institutionalized Presidency: A Conceptual Clarification." In Norman Thomas, ed., *The Presidency in Contemporary Context.* New York: Dodd, Mead, pp. 147–59.

Greenberg, George D. 1980. "Constraints of Management and Secretarial Behavior at HEW." *Polity* 13:57–79.

Greenstein, Fred I. 1979. "Change and Continuity in the Modern Presidency." In Anthony King, ed., *The New American Political System.* Washington, D.C.: American Enterprise Institute, pp. 45–86.

————. 1982. *The Hidden-Hand Presidency: Eisenhower as Leader*. New York: Basic Books.

Heclo, Hugh. 1977. *A Government of Strangers: Executive Politics in Washington*. Washington, D.C.: Brookings Institution.

————. 1979. "Issue Networks and the Executive Establishment." In A. King, ed., *The New American Political System*. Washington, D.C.: American Enterprise Institute, pp. 87–124.

————. 1983. "One Executive Branch or Many?" In Anthony King, ed., *Both Ends of the Avenue: The President, the Executive Branch, and Congress in the 1980's*. Washington, D.C.: American Enterprise Institute, pp. 26–58.

Herman, Valentine, and James E. Alt, eds. 1975. *Cabinet Studies: A Reader*. New York: St. Martin's.

Hess, Stephen. 1976. *Organizing the Presidency*. Washington, D.C.: Brookings Institution.

Hibbing, John R. 1982a. *Retirement from the House*. Washington, D.C.: University Press of America.

————. 1982b. "Voluntary Retirement from the U.S. House: The Cost of Congressional Service." *Legislative Studies Quarterly* 7:57–74.

Horn, Stephen J. 1960. *The Cabinet and Congress*. New York: Columbia University Press.

Hoxie, R. Gordon. 1984. The Cabinet in the American Presidency, 1789–1984." *Presidential Studies Quarterly* 14:209–31.

Huntington, Samuel P. 1968. *Political Order in Changing Societies*. New Haven, Conn.: Yale University Press.

————. 1973. "Congressional Responses to the Twentieth Century." In D. Truman, ed., *Congress and America's Future*. 2d ed. Englewood Cliffs, N.J.: Prentice-Hall, pp. 6–38.

Jewell, Malcolm E. 1982. *Representation in State Legislatures*. Lexington: University Press of Kentucky.

Kemp, Kathleen A. 1983. "The Regulators: Partisanship and Public Policy." *Policy Studies Journal* 3:386–97.

Kesselman, Mark. 1970. "Overinstitutionalization and Political Constraint." *Comparative Politics* 3:21–44.

Kessler, Frank. 1982. *The Dilemmas of Presidential Leadership: Of Caretakers and Kings*. Englewood Cliffs, N.J.: Prentice-Hall.

Key, V. O. 1955. "A Theory of Critical Elections." *Journal of Politics* 17:3–18.

King, James D., and James W. Riddlesperger, Jr. 1984. "Presidential Cabinet Appointments: The Partisan Factor." *Presidential Studies Quarterly* 14:231–37.

Kingdon, John W. 1984. *Agendas, Alternatives, and Public Policies*. Boston: Little, Brown.

Krislov, Samuel, and David H. Rosenbloom. 1981. *Representative Bureaucracy and the American Political System*. New York: Praeger.

Laski, Harold J. 1940. *The American Presidency: An Interpretation*. New York: Harper and Brothers.

Lasswell, Harold. 1948. "Skill Politics and Skill Revolution." In *The Analysis of Political Behavior*. New York: Oxford University Press, pp. 133–45.

Lasswell, Harold, and Daniel Lerner, eds. 1965. *World Revolutionary Elites: Studies in Coercive Ideological Movements*. Cambridge, Mass.: MIT Press.

Light, Paul, C. 1983. "The Institutional Vice Presidency." *Presidential Studies Quarterly* 13: 198–211.

Lowi, Theodore J. 1964. *At the Pleasure of the Mayor*. New York: Free Press.

———. 1969. *The End of Liberalism*. New York: Norton.

McDonald, Forrest. 1974. *The Presidency of George Washington*. New York: Norton.

Mackenzie, G. Calvin. 1981. *The Politics of Presidential Appointments*. New York: Free Press.

Mann, Dean, with Jameson Doig. 1965. *The Assistant Secretaries: Problems and Processes of Appointment*. Washington, D.C.: Brookings Institution.

Mann, Dean, and Zachary Smith. 1981. "The Selection of U.S. Cabinet Officers and Other Political Executives." *International Political Science Review* 2:211–34.

Matthews, Donald R. 1954. *The Social Background of Political Decision-Makers*. New York: Random House.

Meier, Kenneth J., and Lloyd G. Nigro. 1976. "Representative Bureaucracy and Policy Preferences: A Study in the Attitudes of Federal Executives." *Public Administration Review* 36:458–69.

Miles, Rufus E. 1978. "A Cabinet Department of Education: An Unwise Campaign Promise or a Sound Idea?" *Public Administration Review* 39:103–10.

Miller, Warren E., and Donald E. Stokes. 1963. "Constituency Influence in Congress." *American Political Science Review* 57:45–56.

Mitnick, Barry M. 1980. *The Political Economy of Regulation*. New York: Columbia University Press.

Moe, Terry M. 1985. "The Politicized Presidency." In J. Chubb and P. Peterson, eds., *The New Direction in American Politics*. Washington, D.C.: Brookings Institution, pp. 235–72.

Mosca, Gaetano. 1939. *The Ruling Class*. New York: McGraw-Hill.

Nathan, Richard P. 1975. *The Plot that Failed: Nixon and the Administrative Presidency*. New York: John Wiley.

———. 1983. *The Administrative Presidency*. New York: John Wiley.

Neustadt, Richard E. 1954. "Presidency and Legislation: The Growth of Central Clearance." *American Political Science Review* 48:641–71.

———. 1955. "Presidency and Legislation: Planning the President's Program." *American Political Science Review* 49:980–1021.

———. 1960. *Presidential Power*. New York: John Wiley.

Newland, Chester. 1983. "A Mid-Term Appraisal—The Reagan Presidency: Limited Government and Political Administration." *Public Administration Review* 43:1–21.

———. 1985. "Executive Office Policy Apparatus: Enforcing the Reagan Agenda." In L. Salamon and M. Lund, eds., *The Reagan Presidency and the Governing of America.* Washington, D.C.: Urban Institute, pp. 135–68.

Norpoth, Helmut, and Jerrold G. Rusk. 1982. "Partisan Dealignment in the American Electorate." *American Political Science Review* 76:522–37.

Pfiffner, James P. 1986. "White House Staff Versus the Cabinet: Centripetal and Centrifugal Roles." *Presidential Studies Quarterly* 16:666–90.

Pious, Richard M. 1979. *The American Presidency.* New York: Basic Books.

Pitkin, Hanna Fenichel. 1967. *The Concept of Representation.* Berkeley and Los Angeles: University of California Press.

Polsby, Nelson W. 1968. "The Institutionalization of the U.S. House of Representatives." *American Political Science Review* 62:144–67.

———. 1977. *Presidential Cabinet Making: Lessons for the Political System.* Bloomington: Poynter Center, Indiana University.

———. 1978. "Presidential Cabinet Making." *Political Science Quarterly* 43:15–26. Reprinted in S. Shull and L. LeLoup, eds., *The Presidency: Studies in Policy Making.* Brunswick, Ohio: King's Court, pp. 83–94.

———. 1983. *Consequences of Party Reform.* New York: Oxford University Press.

Prewitt, Kenneth, and William McAllister. 1976. "Changes in the American Executive Elite, 1930–1970." In H. Eulau and M. Czudnowski, eds., *Elite Recruitment in Democratic Politics.* New York: Sage, pp. 105–32.

Price, Don K. 1983. *America's Unwritten Constitution: Science, Religion, and Political Responsibility.* Baton Rouge: Louisiana State University Press.

Putnam, Robert D. 1976. *The Comparative Study of Political Elites.* Englewood Cliffs, N.J.: Prentice-Hall.

Randall, Ronald. 1979. "Presidential Power versus Bureaucratic Intransigence: The Influence of the Nixon Administration on Welfare Policy." *American Political Science Review* 73: 795–810.

Riddlesperger, James W. 1986. "Senate Confirmation of Presidential Administrative Appointments: The Carter and Reagan Years." Presented at the 1986 Southern Political Science Association meeting.

Rieselbach, Leroy N. 1977. *Congressional Reform in the Seventies.* Morristown, N.J.: General Learning Press.

Schlesinger, Joseph A. 1966. *Ambition and Politics.* Chicago: Rand McNally.

Seidman, Harold. 1980. *Politics, Position, and Power: The Dynamics of Federal Organization.* 3d ed. New York: Oxford University Press.

Seligman, Lester G. 1967. "Presidential Leadership: The Inner Circle and Institutionalization." *Journal of Politics* 18:410–26.

Sobel, Robert, ed. 1977. *Biographical Directory of the United States Executive Branch.* 2d ed. Westport, Conn.: Greenwood.

Stanley, David T., Dean E. Mann, and James W. Doig. 1967. *Men Who Govern.* Washington, D.C.: Brookings Institution.

Subramanian, V. 1969. "Representative Bureaucracy." *American Political Science Review* 61:1010–19.

Verba, Sidney, and Norman Nie. 1972. *Participation in America.* New York: Harper and Row.

Wahlke, John C. 1978. "Policy Demands and System Support: The Role of the Represented." In H. Eulau and J. Wahlke, eds. *The Politics of Representation: Continuities in Theory and Research.* Beverly Hills, Calif.: Sage, pp. 73–90.

Walker, Walter Earl, and Michael R. Reopel. 1984. "The Extended Presidential Transition: Policy Making and Cabinet Government in the Reagan Administration." Presented at the 1984 Southern Political Science Association meeting.

Weisband, Edward, and Thomas M. Frank. 1975. *Resignation in Protest.* New York: Grossman.

Weisberg, Herbert F. 1980. "Cabinet Transfers and Department Prestige." Presented at the 1980 Midwest Political Science Association meeting.

Wilson, Graham K. 1977. "Are Department Secretaries Really a President's Natural Enemy?" *British Journal of Political Science* 7:272–99. Reprinted in Harry A. Bailey, ed., *Classics of the American Presidency.* Oak Park, Ill.: Moore Publishing, 1980, pp. 134–50.

Witmer, Richard T. 1964. "The Aging of the House." *Political Science Quarterly* 79: 526–41.

Wyszomirski, Margaret Jane. 1982. "The De-Institutionalization of Presidential Staff Agencies." *Public Administration Review* 42:448–58.

Young, James S. 1966. *The Washington Community, 1800–1828.* New York: Columbia University Press.

INDEX

Pitt Series in Policy and Institutional Studies
Bert A. Rockman, Editor